First-Year Harmony

First-Year

HARMONY

Philip Friedheim

The Free Press, New York
Collier-Macmillan Limited, London

This book is dedicated to

Larry and Sue, David, Liz, Mick, Pamela, and Cindy,

who taught me how to teach

PREFACE

First-Year Harmony is designed primarily to be read at home, and discussed in class. Each section is followed by appropriate exercises, which are, of course, absolutely vital. Notwithstanding the general title of "music theory," we are always very much involved in the "practice." Music is not merely something one listens to and talks about; it is something one does something about. One must not only learn facts and figures, but genuine skills as well. It is not possible to understand the theory of music without having struggled with the material itself.

Perhaps this text differs from others in that it is specifically designed to be *read*. It tends to avoid an objective presentation of information, and more often than not approaches its problems as areas to be explored and possibilities to be considered. Thus it is full of speculation and suggestion. Ideally, it should be as intriguing as the subject itself.

The general approach is fundamentally historical. Tonality evolved over a period of time, reached its fruition at a certain point in history, and affected the style of certain composers. I have continually tried to relate the technical information to the actual compositions of the 18th and 19th centuries, not merely by choosing examples from these works, but by continually referring to the music of Bach and Mozart for examination.

I am convinced that this is more exciting and more meaningful than an incidental quotation of two or three bars taken out of context.

Many exercises are suggested throughout the text. These should be written in the Workbook, which not only affords a neat format for copying, but supplies extra exercises as well. Some of these will train the student in essential skills; others might or might not be used at the discretion of the teacher; many could be completed by an ambitious pupil working by himself. To use the Workbook to its best advantage, the student should work out all assignments on scrap paper first, and only after they are completed to his satisfaction should they be copied (*in pencil*) into the Workbook. From the very beginning, the teacher should insist that all assignments be neat, that clefs be drawn properly, that stems move in the right direction, etc.

The assignments tend to differ from those appearing in more formal textbooks. Here, I agree with Arnold Schoenberg in deploring the traditional approach of giving students melodies to harmonize. As Schoenberg says, "Harmonizing given melodies is in contradiction to the process of composition; a composer invents melody and harmony simultaneously." I also follow Schoenberg in another way, as I start the student composing chord progressions as soon as possible. In following some of Schoenberg's methods, however, I have never chosen to ignore other approaches. The exercises stress individual composition (one tries something out and sees what happens) and analysis (one examines the works of the great composers and asks questions about their procedures). The student must continually live with this music on the most meaningful terms. Our tools of perception are never sharp enough.

In writing the text, I have presupposed from the beginning that the student can read music. I have not included sight-singing or dictation exercises: suffice it to say that at any stage in a student's development he should be able to hear what he sees on the page, and to know what the music he hears would look like if it were written out. Although this area of instruction is vital, a textbook may not supply the most adequate guide. To some extent this material should be selected to fit the individual needs of the student.

Although my name appears alone as the author of this work, I have certainly been helped by a number of people in a variety of ways. First, my own students have helped me, and I have thanked some of them in the dedication. Next, I must thank Mr. Frederick Freedman, who first suggested the idea of writing this book, and made numerous suggestions about the manuscript itself. Then, I owe a strong debt of gratitude to Mr. Edward McLeroy at Free Press for his endless patience with my delays over these past three years. For numerous specific points throughout the text I am generally indebted to my colleagues and teachers, most specifically to Dr. Harry Lincoln, who read the entire manuscript and offered many helpful suggestions. Next, I must thank Prof. William Kimmel. I could never write anything about music without acknowledging all he has taught me, both in and out of the classroom, these past fifteen years. Finally, my warmest thanks are extended to my wife Valerie for her patience and indulgence on those frequent evenings and Saturdays that were needed for the completion of this book. I am sure she knows that nothing was taken away, since in the largest sense everything belongs to her.

I acknowledge with thanks the following: Harvard University Press for the music excerpts used in my Examples 1, 2, and 3 (Apel and Davison, *Historical Anthology of Music,* Vol. 1). G. Shirmer, Inc. for an excerpt from Schoenberg's Piano Concerto, Op. 42. Elkan-Vogel Co. for an excerpt from Ravel's *Ma Mère l'Oye.* (Permission granted for reprint by

Durand & Cie, Paris, copyright owners; Elkan-Vogel Co., Inc., Philadelphia, Agents.) Boosey and Hawkes Inc. for an excerpt from Richard Strauss' *Ariadne auf Naxos*. Theodore Presser Company for excerpts from Alban Berg's *Lyric Suite* (Universal Edition, 1900, used by permission) and Anton Webern's *Five Canons* (Universal Edition, 1900, used by permission). And to Mrs. Gertrude Schoenberg for her gracious permission to use an excerpt from Schoenberg's *Verklärte Nacht,* Op. 4.

Philip Friedheim

CONTENTS

PART I

Introduction to
Diatonic Harmony

1

THE HERITAGE OF
WESTERN MUSIC

Music, often called the international language, is at the same time the most useless of all the arts. While it can be highly expressive, it cannot express anything in particular, even though it may suggest a story or include a vocal text. It exists fundamentally by and for itself. Volumes have been written attempting to define what music expresses, and as many volumes have been written proving these definitions wrong. No one can reveal the specific content of music, or explain why it should be so appealing. Those of us who have once come under the spell of a great musical masterpiece will certainly never forget it, although we would find it difficult to state exactly what we have experienced.

At the depths of this mystery lies the fact that music is not merely appealing or attractive (actually, many fine compositions can be violent and dramatic); music is a vital and necessary part of human life. One should remember that virtually no civilization has existed without it. Anthropologists and sociologists continually note that tribes throughout the world, in spite of the most primitive living conditions and the most desperate struggles to survive, invariably find time for music.

It accompanies them at work and at prayer, in grief and in play, in groups or alone.

It is interesting to study the music of different civilizations. This is the job of the ethnomusicologist. We, however, will be concerned primarily with the music of our own culture. Many centuries of tradition come under the general heading we call Western Civilization. This heritage, as separate from the ancient worlds of Greece and Rome as it is from the cultures of Asia and Africa, first comes into being in central Europe in the Middle Ages. Covering a span of over 1500 years, it represents some of the highest achievements of man. The music of Western Civilization is greater and more magnificent than the music of any ethnic culture for two very special reasons, the first having to do with notation, the second with harmony. Let us consider both these items separately.

Musical Notation

Siamese bell orchestras can play very complex music; Chinese operas are often long and involved; they demand extraordinarily skillful performers. But since these singers and instrumentalists never work from written music, they are forced to memorize their parts. These are passed on orally from teacher to pupil. As a result, the music tends to remain the same through the centuries, and for each new composition added another is presumably discarded and forgotten. As far as we can tell without historical records, styles do not appear to change or evolve. If they do, those of the past become irrevocably lost.

In our culture, we are aware that the music of Bach (born in 1685) does not sound like that of Brahms (born in 1833). We enjoy the contrast between their styles, and allow the music of different centuries to speak to our different selves. We are so sophisticated historically that we can even tell when Stravinsky deliberately imitates the style of another era. Unlike the Siamese, we are aware of change and evolution, and rejoice as each new generation contributes its own style rather than reiterating that of the past.

The sense of history we gain in this way is safeguarded by our musical notation. Because Bach wrote his music down on paper, we know what it should sound like, and can compare it to that of Brahms. This system of notation enables us to reconstruct and perform a masterpiece like Mozart's *Don Giovanni* with considerable accuracy, even though this opera was composed approximately 200 years ago.

Harmony

The problem of harmony and the way in which it enriches the music of our Western heritage is much more complicated. The compositions of most ancient cultures are primarily *monophonic* (the word *monophony* means literally "one voice"). This means that they consist of individual melodies without accompaniment. They may be very ornate, and may contain unusual rhythms, but they utilize only one note at a time. All performers, vocalists and instrumentalists, sound the same notes together. Occasionally, some of the performers may vary the melody slightly while others play it undecorated. The result is now *heterophonic* (the word *heterophony* means literally "other voices"). Even here, however, where different notes occasionally occur at the same time, there still remains one essential melody. The departures introduced by the performers appear only momentarily.

In Western music, on the other hand, the possibilities of

harmony have been consistently employed for over 1000 years. The discovery that different notes can be sounded "harmoniously" at the same time has given a richness and depth to our music beyond all the unusual melodies, exotic scales, and colorful orchestrations of monophonic music. Our music is fundamentally *polyphonic* (the word *polyphony* means literally "many voices"). The art of *counterpoint,* the combination of separate voices performing different melodies simultaneously, demands a great deal of skill on the part of the composer.

The notation we use today took centuries to evolve into its present form. Despite this, it is not difficult to learn to read, since the staffs, clefs, and rhythmic signs form part of a logical and systematic pattern. The possibilities of harmony, on the other hand, are much more complicated, and considerably more difficult to learn. At the same time, a knowledge of harmony is of fundamental importance to every musician. It is invaluable on the practical as well as the theoretical level. It clarifies the nature of the stylistic changes in the various historical periods; it helps reveal the structure and meaning of music; it establishes the fundamental material for the composer, arranger, and teacher. The performer cannot properly interpret his music, nor can he create appropriate embellishments or cadenzas without a knowledge of harmony. In a real sense, the study of harmony is the study of Western music.

EXERCISE

Define the following terms:
        Monophony
        Heterophony
        Polyphony
        Ethnomusicology
        Counterpoint
        Harmony

2

TONALITY AND HARMONY

THE DISCOVERY OF HARMONY was made early in the Middle
Ages. No one knows exactly how this phenomenon came about.
It probably started as an elaborate outgrowth of heterophony:
one musician lavishly improvising around the original melody.
Eventually, these improvisations became codified and notated.
Example 1 is a passage from a monophonic church chant
composed in the early centuries of the Christian era.

EXAMPLE 1

Do   -   -   -   mi – no

Example 2 (page 20) is the beginning of the same passage as it
appears in a two-part polyphonic setting from the early twelfth
century. Note that the first five notes of the original melody
appear in the lower voice.

This type of single part-singing, known as *organum,* was
in practice by the tenth century. At that time, music was
still primarily monophonic, and organum was considered a
decoration to the original melody. As the examples 1 and 2
demonstrate, there was no known method of notating the

rhythm. Because of this, polyphony did not develop beyond a very limited point since the performers would have had difficulty keeping together if the separate parts were to become too independent.

EXAMPLE 2

In the twelfth century, when a method of rhythmic notation was finally achieved, polyphony came into its own as an art form. This monumental step first appeared in the organum written for the services at Notre Dame in Paris. Example 3 is a portion of the chant in a polyphonic setting. Again, the original melody appears in the lower voice.

EXAMPLE 3

Even though this fragment might appear to be more "musical" than the preceding one, it certainly does not sound like the sort of music we normally hear in the concert hall today. From the twelfth to the twentieth century, styles of harmony changed often and radically. Combinations of notes considered acceptable at one time were unacceptable at another.

Composers initially concerned with discovering which notes could be sounded together later became more aware of musical movement and *harmonic direction*. Certain tones tended to dominate the melodic pattern and to draw other notes toward them; certain harmonic combinations created tensions which could be relieved by moving the notes in specified ways. By the end of the seventeenth century the elaborate harmonic system known as *tonality* was completely formed. Tonality basically defines a set of relationships connecting all musical notes to each other. These notes revolve around a central keynote in much the same manner as the planets revolve around the sun. Thus, when we speak of "the key of F," we have simply identified the central note. Some of the remaining notes will lie close to this center, while others will be more distant. Just as the gravitational force of the sun controls the movements of the various planets, so the central position of the keynote controls the movements of the other notes.

Tonality was not a sudden invention; it evolved slowly over the centuries as composers became more aware of the relationships existing between tones. As a result, it is impossible to draw an absolute line between the music of the late seventeenth century, which is truly tonal, and the music immediately preceding that time, which is not. A general date of approximately 1680 can be set, with Arcangelo Corelli as perhaps the first composer to write music that consistently remained within a clear tonal frame.

The span of time during which tonality reigned supreme extended through the end of the nineteenth century and concluded with the works of Wagner and Brahms. Finally, by 1909 Arnold Schoenberg disrupted this concept that had held forth for over 200 years. Despite the appearance of Schoenberg's "atonal" (without tonality) compositions, however, tonality continues to attract many composers.

During the tonal period (ca. 1680–1910), musical styles

changed often, although the fundamental harmonies never altered radically. Brahms' music was composed 150 years after that of Bach, yet there is very little in Brahms that would have been incomprehensible to Bach. On the other hand, if Bach could have looked back 100 years, or if Brahms could have looked forward even 50 years, they would have discovered harmonic practices that might have surprised them.

As short-lived as it actually was in view of the entire history of Western music, the period of tonality remains particularly significant for present-day musicians. It was certainly the longest period since the beginning of polyphony in which one fundamental system of harmony was used. In addition, composers who wrote in this system continue to supply most of the music performed in the concert halls today. With the single exception of opera, most of the forms we associate with serious music arose soon after tonality became established; the symphony was created in the eighteenth century, along with the solo sonata and concerto as we know them, chamber music, piano music, the art song, etc. Although many masterpieces were created in the years before and after tonality held sway, they lie outside our special interest for the present.

During the historical period of tonality, the changes in musical styles divided the era into at least four clearly defined periods. These are usually designated as follows: (1) the late Baroque, lasting from approximately 1680 to 1750; (2) the Classical period, from approximately 1750 to 1800; (3) the Romantic period, extending through the nineteenth century; and (4) the post-Romantic period, overlapping into the twentieth century. Some of the major composers are listed below.

I. *Late Baroque* (ca. 1680–1750)
    Arcangelo Corelli (1653–1713)
    Antonio Vivaldi (1675–1743)
    Johann Sebastian Bach (1685–1750)

Domenico Scarlatti (1685–1757)
George Frederic Handel (1685–1759)
II. *Classical* (ca. 1750–1800)
Franz Joseph Haydn (1732–1809)
Wolfgang Amadeus Mozart (1756–1791)
Ludwig van Beethoven (1770–1827)
III. *Romantic* (ca. 1800–1890)
Franz Schubert (1797–1828)
Hector Berlioz (1803–1869)
Frederick Chopin (1810–1845)
Robert Schumann (1810–1856)
Franz Liszt (1811–1886)
Richard Wagner (1813–1883)
Giuseppi Verdi (1813–1901)
Johannes Brahms (1833–1897)
Peter Tchaikovsky (1840–1893)
IV. *Post-Romantic* (ca. 1890–1910)
Gustav Mahler (1860–1911)
Claude Debussy (1862–1918)
Richard Strauss (1864–1948)
Maurice Ravel (1875–1937)

Unfortunately, the stylistic differences between these periods cannot be analyzed here in detail. As the student becomes familiar with the music, however, he will have no difficulty in identifying the proper periods, even for compositions he hears for the first time. As far as the harmony is concerned, the Baroque and Romantic periods are more complex than the Classical period. In the Post-Romantic period, the harmony became so complex that tonality began to disintegrate. All the major post-Romantic composers tended to move beyond the limits of the tonal system.

Define the following terms:
    Tonality
    Atonality
    Organum

In addition to the names mentioned in the chapter, name five composers who wrote tonal music, five who wrote before tonality was established, and five who wrote after tonality had been abandoned.

PART II

Fundamental Materials
of Tonality

3

SOUNDS, PITCHES, SCALES, AND KEYS

Sounds and Pitches

THE BASIC MATERIAL of music is sound. The composition of music is the organization of sound within time. In examining this basic material, we can distinguish between two different types of sounds: those with a definite pitch, and those without a definite pitch.

Sound is created through the vibration of an object, for example the string of a piano or a violin. If it vibrates fast enough, the ear can detect these movements as sound. A sound has a definite pitch when it maintains a consistent number of vibrations per second. Thus, the note called "concert A," to which symphony orchestras tune, is normally set at 440 vibrations per second. As the number of vibrations increases, the pitch becomes higher. Most orchestral instruments, including all the strings. woodwinds, and brasses, produce definite pitches.

In certain cases, however, vibrations become confused or inconsistent, producing no specific pitch. Technically speaking, these sounds are classified as noise. Many percussion instruments, such as the bass drum, gong, snare drum, and triangle, do not produce definite pitches.

Physicists can build electronic machines capable of sounding any number of vibrations per second. There is one difficulty however, while the machine is quite accurate, the human ear is not. A normal person has a distinctly limited hearing ability. He cannot normally detect vibrations lower than 20 per second, nor higher than 20,000.[1] Furthermore, the ear cannot discriminate between minute changes in pitch. The difference between a tone produced at 200 vibrations and another produced at 201 vibrations can hardly be detected even by a trained musician. It is only after the number of vibrations have increased considerably that a listener will be able to notice the change. When a singer or violinist is said to be "sharp" or "flat," or that a piano is "out of tune"—it means, technically, that the number of vibrations is slightly more or less than it should be in order to be "on pitch." The difference is noticeable even though the note remains substantially the same. Eventually, however, when the pitch varies sufficiently, we hear a distinctly new tone. Middle C on the piano is produced by approximately 261.5 vibrations per second, the C♯ directly above it by 277. The C above middle C has 523 vibrations, or exactly twice that of the lower octave. This two-to-one ratio undoubtedly accounts for the close relationship between all notes an octave apart.

People in African and Asian cultures are quite sensitive to minute gradations of pitch, but in Western cultures we have set an absolute pattern to distinguish our notes. The smallest acceptable difference between two notes is called a half step or half tone. (The notes of the piano keyboard are constructed in half steps.) The distance between C and C♯, as well as the distance between C♯ and D, is a half step. The difference between C and D then becomes a whole step, since it contains two half-steps.

[1] These figures are not absolute, since the audible range of sound varies considerably with different individuals, and actually decreases as a person ages.

Scales and Keys

One must always remember that the various notes form sets of relationships with each other. As a result of these relationships, certain pitches become interconnected. Thus, when a singer or a composer invents a melody, he does not simply move at random among all the possible sounds. He actually uses a small number of tones, returning to them again and again. In this way his melody achieves unity and coherence. The specific collection of pitches used in a melody is called a scale.

One example will demonstrate how a scale is formed, and how the notes relate to each other. The melody of the hymn *America* contains 41 notes set to 39 syllables of text. When we look closely, however, we find that these notes actually use only a very small number of different pitches.

EXAMPLE 4

The six notes used actually contain only three pitches: E, F, and G. The F is used three times, the G twice. The next two phrases (ten notes) introduce only two new pitches: A and B♭.

EXAMPLE 5

If we arrange these five pitches in order from the lowest to the highest, we can see that the first three phrases of the song are based on a scale using E, F, G, A, and B♭. Even within these five notes, a clear set of relationships is discernable. F is the most important note of all, since it appears more times than any of the others. It opens the melody, and it ends the second and third phrases.

The fourth and fifth phrases move away from F, but within their twelve notes only one new pitch, C, is added.

EXAMPLE 6

The last two phrases rise to the highest note of all, D, and then move back to complete the hymn on the original F.

EXAMPLE 7

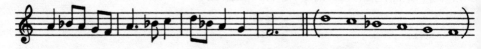

Thus, through careful examination, we have seen that the 41 notes comprising the melody *America* only use seven different pitches: E, F, G, A, Bb, C, and D, all of them either a whole step or a half step apart from their nearest neighbors. We have also seen that the F is the most important note of the group. Translating these observations into musical terminology, we can say that the melody is in the key of F, and that it is built on the F-major scale. The keynote is often called the *tonic,* since it is the central tone. When we spell out the notes of the scale, we traditionally start with the keynote and move upward to the same pitch an octave higher.[2] The F-major scale is found in example 8.

[2] Why do we repeat the opening keynote once again at the top of the scale? The student should try playing the scale and stopping after the seventh note. The effect is quite unsatisfying. The keynote has such a strong magnetic pull that the scale, theoretically complete with its seven pitches, sounds unfinished until it comes to rest back on the tonic.

EXAMPLE 8

Remember, we began with a melody, and from the notes of the melody extracted the underlying scale. The scale as such was not played during the song. Only through analysis can one isolate the pitches and form the scale. Thus, the composer does not invent a scale, and then write a melody; he begins with a melody. The scale is only an abstract concept that may or may not appear in the music.

EXERCISE

Using *America* as a guide (since we know it begins on the keynote), reconstruct the same melody beginning on C, and then, when this is completed, write out the C-major scale. Using the same melody, find the scales of D, E, G, and A. As a guide, write all the "black notes" as sharps rather than flats (i.e., F♯, not G♭). Otherwise, the notes will not be properly arranged into a scale. (Workbook, Section I, Exercises 4–13)

Be sure you know the meaning of the following terms:

Music
Sound
Pitch
Noise
Concert A
Half step
Whole step
Scale
Key
Tonic

Make a list of those musical instruments that have a definite pitch, and those that do not. (Workbook, Section I, Exercises 2, 3)

Find the scale for the following melodies: *Over the Rainbow, Swanee River.* (Workbook, Section I, Exercises 14, 15)

4

THE STRUCTURE OF
THE MAJOR SCALE

THIS CHAPTER will be devoted to the major scale as an abstract entity, the following chapter to the relationship of the scale to the melodies from which it is derived.

We have already seen that *America* can be played in a variety of keys starting on C, D, E, F, G, and A. The notes may be different, but in each case the melody sounds the same. It is obvious that these scales are quite similar to each other. Our system of tuning supplies us with twelve separate pitches, each spaced a half step apart. In the seven-note scale, some of the pitches are a half step apart, while others are a whole step apart. If we number each step of the scale, we can see exactly where the differences appear. Let us compare the three scales of C, D, and E.

In each case, we note a whole step interval between all notes except the third and fourth, and the seventh and eighth. In both these places, the distance is only a half step. The position of the two half steps provides the most significant clue to the construction of the major scale.

EXAMPLE 9

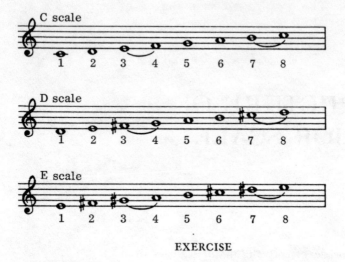

EXERCISE

Check the G and A scales to see whether they contain the same half steps in the same places. In the Workbook (Section 1, Exercises 11, 13) where the scales have already been written, the distance between each step should be identified, and a slur placed between the half steps.

Without using the melody of *America,* construct a scale beginning on B, using the proper order of whole steps and half steps as a guide. (Workbook, Section II, Exercise 1)

Now it should be clear why in these cases the "black notes" must be written as sharps. If you move a whole step from I to II [1] in the key of B, you must move from B to C♯, not from B to D♭, even though C♯ and D♭ are the same notes on the piano. If you were to write D♭ for the second note, some form of the letter C would be omitted, and the scale would run out of letters before it was completed.

[1] The steps in scale are always indicated by Roman numbers, since, as we shall see later, Arabic numbers have a different function in the study of harmony.

34

Now that the proper distance between each note of the scale is known, a major scale can be constructed beginning on any note, using sharps and flats as the notation requires.

EXERCISE

Complete the construction of all twelve scales in the following manner:

1. Construct scales on A♭ and B♭ building up from the keynote.

2. Construct scales on D♭ and E♭ moving down. In other words, instead of progressing from I to II to III, use the keynote as VIII, and then move down the proper distance to VII, VI, etc.

3. As a final exercise in scale construction, build a major scale upward from F♯, and then, spelling the same note as G♭, build the identical scale downward.[2] These two scales will use the same notes on the piano, but they will be notated in a completely different manner. (Workbook, Section II, Exercises 2–8)

Now that we have finally completed all twelve major scales (actually thirteen, if the enharmonic F♯-G♭ is counted twice), we can begin to perceive a larger pattern binding all the keys together. Note that each of these scales contains a different number of sharps and flats, and that no major scale combines sharps and flats together. Only one scale contains neither sharps nor flats: the so-called white note scale of C. Only one scale contains one sharp, another two sharps, another three sharps, etc. The same is true for the flats. One never finds a situation where a major scale contains only one flat on one note, while another scale contains only one flat but on a different note.

---

[2] A change in the musical spelling of a note while the pitch remains the same, as in this case where F♯ = G♭, is called an *enharmonic change*.

The only key containing one flat is the key of F, and that flat is always B, just as we first noticed it in *America*.

If we take all the scales, separate those using sharps from those using flats, and arrange them in order starting with those having the least number of accidentals,[3] the result will look like this:

Key of C   – no sharps
Key of G   – 1 sharp: F
Key of A   – 2 sharps: F, C
Key of D   – 3 sharps: F, C, G
Key of E   –4 sharps: F, C, G, D
Key of B   – 5 sharps: F, C, G, D, A
Key of F♯ – 6 sharps: F, C, G, D, A, E

Key of C   – no flats
Key of F   – 1 flat: B
Key of B♭ – 2 flats: B, E
Key of E♭ – 3 flats: B, E, A
Key of A♭ – 4 flats: B, E, A, D
Key of D♭ – 5 flats: B, E, A, D, G
Key of G♭– 6 flats: B, E, A, D, G, C

Both sets of sharp and flat keys begin with the same key, C, and both end with the same key, the enharmonic F♯–G♭. Thus, the complete set of scales forms a single unit, a large circle in which each key is placed between two others that differ from it either through the addition or subtraction of one sharp or flat.

This diagram is also known as the circle of fifths. If one begins on any note and moves clockwise, the next keynote will always be five notes higher (include both keynotes in the

---

[3] Any sign placed in front of a written note to alter the pitch, i.e., a flat (♭), sharp (♯), or natural (♮), is called an *accidental*.

count). Continuing up these fifths, one eventually traverses all twelve notes and returns to the original one.

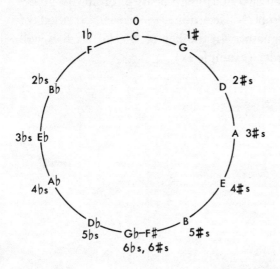

If a composer writes a composition in the key of F♯ major, where six of his seven notes are raised, he certainly does not place a sharp in front of all these notes throughout the entire work. Rather, he places the appropriate number of sharps at the very left of the staff *in their proper order*.

EXAMPLE 10

This, then, is the key signature, and to anyone familiar with the circle of fifths it clearly indicates the major scale and the tonic keynote for the composition. If the music is written in the key of G, only the first sharp will be used; if it is in the key of D, the first two sharps will be used. From this guide, the student can properly determine the correct method of writing each key signature. In the key of Gb, the six flats will be written in this order (example 11).

EXAMPLE 11

EXERCISE

As a final summary, travel clockwise around the circle of fifths, beginning with C, and construct each of the thirteen scales, following each with its appropriate signature. (Workbook, Section II, Exercise 9) Much of this has been done before, and can be copied over. Nevertheless, this exercise is of inestimable value, for if written carefully, it can be used as a reference throughout the course of study, or at least until the entire series has been memorized. Each scale should be written in the following manner:

EXAMPLE 12

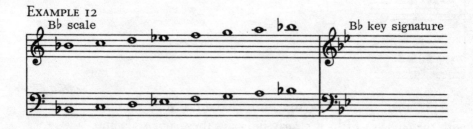

Define the following terms:
    Major scale
    Enharmonic change
    Accidental
    Circle of fifths
    Key signature

5

MORE ABOUT SCALES

Other Scales

Up to this time, we have considered only one type of scale, which is called "major." There are, of course, many other types of scales, the most important, after the major, being the "minor." The differences between these scales lie in the position of the half steps and whole steps. It has been noted that in the major scale the half steps occur between the third and fourth, and between the seventh and eighth notes. These half steps appear in different places in other scales.

The major and minor scales stand apart from all other scale patterns because they are the only two that are *tonal*. In other words, during the period from 1680 to 1910, these were virtually the only scales used in Western music. In addition to tonal scales, however, there are innumerable combinations of notes for different types of melodies. Ethnic cultures use many unusual scales. People whose music shows little awareness of harmony often develop subtle scales and complex rhythmic figures. Folk songs often employ these scales. Finally, much of the music of our own civilization written before 1680 or after 1910 uses other than the major and minor scales. In all these cases, however, they do not produce compositions employing an absolute tonality. Only the major and minor scales were used as the basis for music written within the tonal period.[1]

Excluding ethnic scales that use tunings smaller than our half step, we can identify some of these non-tonal scales. The first, and perhaps most important, in the twelve-note combination consisting of all the half step intervals: the chromatic scale. Traditionally, when we write the *ascending* chromatic scale, we notate it with sharps, using flats when the scale *descends*.

EXAMPLE 13

Chromatic scale

After the twelve-note chromatic scale, there are most commonly found a large group of seven-note scales. These consist of various arrangements of five whole steps and two half steps: the diatonic scales. Among these can be found the major and minor scales. The other combinations are called modes, the names of which are taken from ancient Greek sources. In the so-called Lydian mode, for example, the half steps occur between four and five, and seven and eight; in the Dorian mode they occur between two and three, and six and seven. The music written in the early Middle Ages was predominantly modal. The church chant found in example 1 uses D as the keynote in the Dorian mode. Here are the most important of the medieval modes listed for reference, with the positions of the half steps noted.

[1] There are a few famous exceptions to this statement, special cases in which a composer turned to an archaic or exotic scale for a specific effect, but these examples only serve to prove the rule.

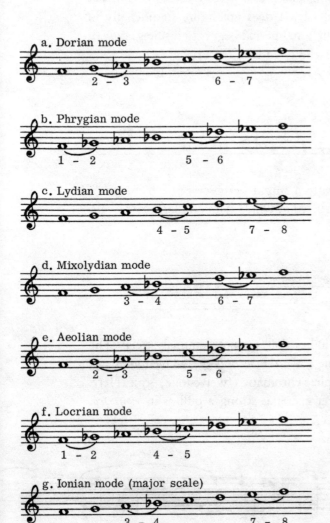

EXAMPLE 14

a. Dorian mode

2 - 3   6 - 7

b. Phrygian mode

1 - 2   5 - 6

c. Lydian mode

4 - 5   7 - 8

d. Mixolydian mode

3 - 4   6 - 7

e. Aeolian mode

2 - 3   5 - 6

f. Locrian mode

1 - 2   4 - 5

g. Ionian mode (major scale)

3 - 4   7 - 8

Another scale, consisting of six notes, can be constructed of equal whole steps throughout. This scale without any half steps seems to have no resting place, and gives the impression that it could continue aimlessly. It does not figure significantly in Western music until the tonal period begins to disintegrate, i.e., until the beginning of the twentieth century.

EXAMPLE 15

Whole tone scale

etc.

Finally, one last pattern might be observed, a five-note or pentatonic scale, constructed of whole steps and larger intervals.

EXAMPLE 16

Pentatonic scale

etc.

Here are three melodies that are not genuinely tonal. The first uses the pentatonic scale, the second the whole-tone scale, and the third the complete chromatic (twelve-tone) scale. Here, a specific keynote never exerts as strong a pull as in *America*.

EXAMPLE 17
a.

44

b.

c.

More About Major Scales

Now let us consider the major scale in its relationship to the
melodies from which it is derived. *America* began and ended
on the same keynote. If the student has tried to "tune out" other
melodies in order to identify their scales, he may already have
run into certain problems. Some of these should be considered,
as they will supply warnings and guides.

Although most melodies end on the tonic, not all melodies
begin there. The magnetic pull of this tone is so strong that a
melody will not sound completely finished unless it returns to
the keynote. In example 18, the Bridal Chorus from Wagner's
Lohengrin has been transposed [2] to the key of C. It does not
begin on the keynote, even though the two opening phrases
both move immediately in that direction.

[2] *Transposition* is the act of shifting a melody from one key to another. The
notes may be different, but the melody will remain the same if the relationship
between the notes is kept constant.

EXAMPLE 18

The melody is in two parts, both of which begin in the same manner. The first part ends on D, and as a result the melody sounds unfinished. When it is repeated, the ending is altered so that it can conclude on C, at which time it does sound completed.

A melody occasionally uses notes that are not a part of its actual scale. These often enhance the expressive quality of the theme, even though they may be only momentary inflections that do not seriously alter the original scale. Example 19, a waltz by Chopin, is transposed to the key of C. However, it includes an F♯ and a C♯ not found in the C-major scale.

EXAMPLE 19

If one added all the notes together as before, one would find a nine-note scale that included both C♮ and C♯, F♮ and F♯. A close inspection, however, will reveal that the two sharps only appear momentarily, and do not affect the position of the key note The first F♯ is immediately cancelled, becoming an F♮ at the very next tone. Thus, the F♯ functions as a *passing note* that moves between the proper scale degrees of G and F. The last F♯ is surrounded on either side by Gs. It acts as a *neighboring note* to the G. Each altered tone, foreign to the key, moves immediately to a note within the key through the shortest possible route, a half step.

The melody can be subjected to one other test. It ends on the proper keynote C, which sounds at this point clearly like the tonic. The appearance of the F♯s might suggest the key of G, since the G scale includes an F♯. The use of both F♯ and C♯ could even suggest the key of D, since that scale uses both these sharps. But notice that the second phrase of this melody ends on a D, and the third phrase ends on a G. Yet in neither place do these notes complete the melody. The waltz is clearly in the key of C, since only that note affords the feeling of complete rest supplied by a tonic. To sum up the characteristics of this melody, one can say that it is written in a diatonic major scale, but contains certain chromatic inflections.

EXAMPLE 20

Thus, we see that it is not always possible to be certain of the scale or the key merely from a quick glance at the melody. Sometimes, when the chromatic inflections become too numerous, it is even difficult for an expert to identify the correct key. Above is a famous example of a melody that uses almost every single half step, the "Habanera" from Bizet's opera

47

Carmen. What do you think is the actual keynote? What are your reasons?

EXERCISE

Transpose the melodies of Wagner's Bridal Chorus (example 18) and Chopin's waltz (Example 19) back into their original keys. The Chorus was written in B♭, the waltz in A♭. Needless to say, this should be done without consulting the printed music. If you know the position of the half steps and whole steps well enough, you can write it out away from the piano keyboard. Then check your result, first by playing it at the piano and listening for errors, and then by consulting a published score of Wagner's *Lohengrin* and of Chopin's *Waltz in A♭*, Op. 69 no. 1. (Workbook, Section III, Exercises 1, 2)

Define:
    Tonal scale
    Chromatic scale
    Mode
    Diatonic scale
    Pentatonic scale
    Whole-tone scale
    Transposition
    Passing note
    Neighbor note
    Chromatic inflection

6

INTERVALS—
RELATIONSHIPS BETWEEN
TWO NOTES

Classifications of Intervals

THE PARTICULAR SCALE used in a composition will affect the relationships between separate notes. Although the scale may never be stated in its bare form within the music, it will supply the underlying basis for the structure. The simplest movement of a melody from one note to another will produce its unique effect depending on the position of these notes in relationship to the tonic. For example, the upward skip from G to C will sound quite different in the key of C from the same skip in the key of G.

In the first version in example 21, the C is the fourth note of the scale. When the melody approaches this note, it continues to move beyond it until it comes to rest on the proper keynote G. In the second example, the C is the tonic, so the melody can satisfactorily end on this pitch.

Let us examine in more detail the effect of the different two-note combinations. Whether the notes are sounded together as a harmony, or successively as a melody, their relationship can be identified by the space or interval between them. The term *interval* is traditionally used to define these distances. Thus, no matter what the key, the interval between G and C will maintain some quality different from that found between G and any other note.

EXAMPLE 21

Key of G

Key of C

In order to number the intervals, we count the lines and spaces between them, *including* both notes. This is done in the following examples, written without a clef.

EXAMPLE 22
Melodic intervals

Harmonic intervals

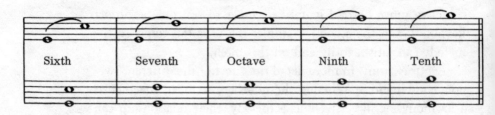

Theoretically, one could continue beyond the 10th, and identify intervals of the 11th, 12th, etc. These notes, however, become so separated from each other after a while that one hardly hears any relationship at all. We tend to interpret widely spaced notes as if they were separate pitches.

It is important to remember that in identifying intervals the number remains constant regardless of accidentals. Thus, any form of C and E is theoretically a 3rd no matter how the notes actually sound.

EXAMPLE 23

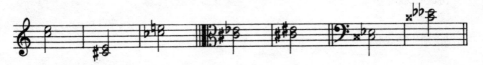

The last interval in example 23 reveals an interesting phenomenon, since both C✕ and E♭♭ sound as D on the piano, Thus, what the ear *hears* as a single note or a unison is *notated* as a 3rd. In this case, one might argue that abstract theoretical possibilities have superseded common sense. In any case, the interval must still be considered a 3rd because it is notated as the distance between some form of C and some form of E. The student might be comforted to learn that the possibility of his finding such an interval in his musical studies is most unlikely.

EXERCISE

With this information as a guide, every interval in examples 17c and 18 should be identified. (Workbook, p. 32)

Families of Intervals.

Having understood the first step in classifying intervals, that of identifying the numerical distance between the notes, we can see that the ten intervals in example 22 do not actually form ten separate categories. Rather, they tend to divide themselves into groups, related not by the size of the interval but by the similarity of the sound produced. If one moves from C up a step to Db, one produces the interval of a 2nd; if one now reverses the procedure, skipping down from C to Db, one produces a 7th; finally, if one moves from C up over an octave to Db, one produces a 9th.[1]

EXAMPLE 24

2nd   7th   9th

Despite the fact that the notes of a 2nd lie close together, while those of a 7th or 9th do not, all three combinations share the same pitches. They will, therefore, share the same sound characteristic: an edge or a bite that produces a certain amount of tension.

Another family of intervals, one with a distinctly different overall quality of sound, contains 3rds, 6ths, and 10ths. As before, these intervals can all be constructed from the same notes: here C and E.

The characteristic sound quality of this group is free of tension, and rather rich and warm. During the eighteenth and nineteenth centuries, the 3rd became the most significant of all

[1] The technical term *inversion* refers to a process where either the upper note of an interval is dropped an octave, or the lower note raised an octave. As a result, the letter notes remain the same, but the distance between them changes.

the harmonic intervals, giving the music of this period its principal harmonic color.

Example 25

3rd   6th   10th

The next family of intervals consists of 4ths and 5ths. These are stronger, colder, and more stark in sound than 3rds and 6ths.

Example 26

5th   4th

Finally, the last identification possible is between unisons and octaves. Here, both intervals can be constructed from the same pitch letter.

Example 27

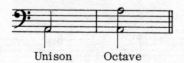

Unison   Octave

In dividing these ten intervals into four separate groups, we have begun to perceive genuine interrelationships between notes. Within each family, the intervals share the same sound characteristics, since they can be constructed from the same notes arranged in different positions. These four groups can be listed as follows:

     1. Unisons and octaves
     2. Seconds, sevenths, and ninths

3. Thirds, sixths, and tenths
4. Fourths and fifths

Practice playing and listening to these intervals until they can be distinguished with ease. For the present, construct all the intervals on the white keys of the piano, using C as the lower note. (Workbook, Section IV, Exercise 1)

Major and Minor Intervals

The first principal category into which intervals can be grouped is determined by noting the distance between the lines and spaces. A second, more specific category denotes the type of interval by counting the number of half steps between the two notes. Thus, the intervals in example 28 are all 2nds, even though some are half steps and some whole steps.

EXAMPLE 28

Whole   Half   Half   Whole
step   step   step   step

Both melodically and harmonically, half steps and whole steps do not sound alike. We traditionally refer to the half step as a minor 2nd and the whole step as a major 2nd. In the major scale, the distance between I and II is a major 2nd, as is the distance between II and III. The distance between III and IV, however, is a minor 2nd.

Example 20 is built almost exclusively from minor 2nds, but be able to identify all ten major 2nds as they appear.

If one can establish a difference between major and minor 2nds, it would follow that the inverted interval, the 7th, can also be divided into major and minor. Again, the larger of the two intervals is major, the smaller one minor. In the major scale, the distance from I up to VII is a major 7th. The same holds true for the 9th.

EXAMPLE 29

Maj 7th   min 7th   Maj 9th   min 9th

When we compare the inversions of these intervals, we find that the major 2nd becomes a minor 7th, and the minor 2nd a major 7th. This rule will hold true in all cases: a minor interval becomes major upon inversion, and vise versa.

EXAMPLE 30

Maj 2   min 7   min 2   Maj 7

When we compare the sound of the major 2nd, C-D, with that of the minor 2nd, C-Db, we notice that despite the difference in intensity, the general characteristic of this entire family, the sharp edge or bite, still remains. The minor 2nd (or major 7th), however, appears to be more dissonant than the major 2nd (or minor 7th).

In a similar manner, the intervals from the next family, 3rds, 6ths, and 10ths, can also be divided into major and minor types. The major 3rd will become a minor 6th on inversion, and the minor 3rd a major 6th. Again, despite the differences in sound, all forms of these intervals maintain the generally warm sonority characteristic of this group.

EXAMPLE 31

M3   m6   m3   M6   M10   m10

Please note in examples 29, 30, and 31 the use of capital "M" for Major and lower case "m" for minor: it is a system often used in the study of harmony.

In summing up these observations, we note that one can divide the intervals in these two families into major and minor types. Either type will maintain some of the characteristic harmonic color of the entire family. A minor interval will become major upon inversion. In the major scale, the distances from I up to II, III, VI, and VII are all major intervals.

EXAMPLE 32

minor 2nd   Major 2nd   minor 3rd   Major 3rd

minor 6th   Major 6th   minor 7th   Major 7th

Practice building each of these intervals from a variety of different notes. Be able to recognize each of these intervals by ear in both their harmonic and melodic forms, ascending as well as descending. Be able to sing any of these intervals in both ascending and descending forms, starting from any given note. (Workbook, Section IV, Exercise 3)

Perfect and Imperfect Intervals

The next two families of intervals are those containing 4ths and 5ths, unisons and octaves. Here again, one can alter the distance between the notes by a half step. In considering these alterations, however, we do not normally speak of major and minor forms, but rather of perfect and imperfect forms. A perfect 4th or 5th appears between I and IV or I and V in the major scale. A perfect interval can be made imperfect in two different ways: by either enlarging or by reducing it a half step. If it is enlarged, it becomes augmented; if reduced, it becomes diminished.

The reasons for the change in terminology from major and minor to perfect and imperfect will become clear as soon as one listens to the sounds. It has been noted that major and minor forms of the same interval maintain the general tone quality of the family from which they come. On the other hand, a considerable difference can be heard between a perfect 5th and a diminished 5th. This difference, in which the elimination of a half step produces a completely different type of sound, is reflected in the names: the perfect interval is invariably stable and solid, while the imperfect forms, the augmented and diminished intervals, are more unstable.

EXAMPLE 33

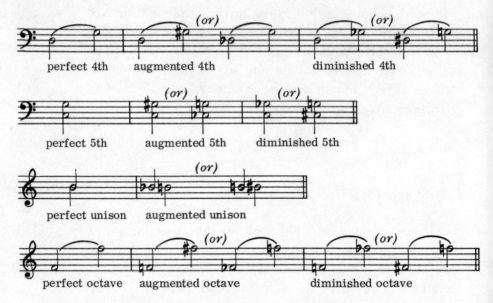

When a major interval is inverted, it becomes minor; when a minor interval is inverted, it becomes major. When an augmented interval is inverted, it becomes diminished, and when a diminished interval is inverted, it becomes augmented. Perfect intervals, however, remain perfect even when they are inverted.

EXAMPLE 34

One can now sum up the preceding observations in the following statements: (1) a major interval becomes minor if it is reduced by a half step; a minor interval becomes major if it is enlarged by a half step. (2) If a perfect interval is expanded by a half step, it becomes augmented; if it is reduced by a half step, it becomes diminished. These two rules can then combine to form the following observation: if a minor interval is reduced again by a half step, it becomes diminished; if a major interval is enlarged by a half step, it will become augmented. One can state this in another way: a major interval can become minor or augmented; a minor interval can become diminished or major, while a perfect interval can become diminished or augmented.

EXAMPLE 35

We will not normally find these theoretical intervals in the average piece of music. Rather, the most stable forms are the most common, while the unusual ones appear infrequently. Example 36 is an organized group of all the most important intervals built on C. It includes every note of the chromatic scale. Note the enharmonic identity of the augmented 4th with the diminished 5th.

The most stable intervals, i. e., the major and perfect forms, exist between C and the other notes of the major scale. These, then, form the diatonic intervals, and will remain basic throughout this study. Next in order of stability are the minor intervals, while diminished and augmented forms remain comparatively uncommon. Example 37 shows the unstable intervals, also built from C. Although infrequently found in tonal music, they must be understood so they can be identified when they do appear.

EXAMPLE 36

EXAMPLE 37

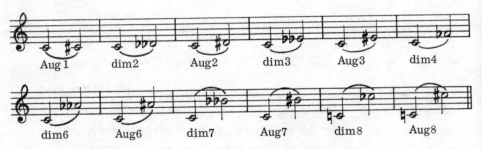

It is not difficult to understand why these intervals do not appear too often. They can only be constructed by employing notes outside of the fundamental scale (including double sharps and flats); they duplicate the sound of the more stable intervals (the diminished 3rd C-E♭♭ is enharmonically identical with the major 2nd C-D); and they often employ enharmonic pitches such as E♯ and C♭. Finally, they cannot be recognized by the ear separated from a musical context.

EXERCISE

Practice until all the intervals in example 36 can be identified by ear, and those in example 37 by sight, in both their melodic and harmonic forms. (Workbook, Section IV, Exercise 4)

Intervals and their Relationship to Melodies

Very often the types of intervals found in certain compositions exert a strong effect on the character of the melodies. We can, for example, distinguish between phrases that move predominantly by steps, i.e., by major and minor 2nds as they are found in scale passages, and others that move predominantly by skips, i.e., by leaps of a 3rd or more. Melodies consisting of many stepwise scale passages are usually easy to sing, and thus appear to be more lyrical in character (see examples 19 and 20).

EXAMPLE 38

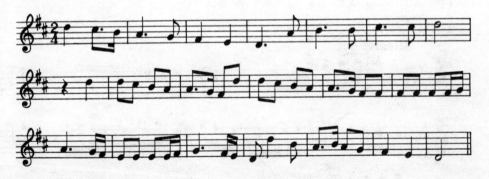

On the other hand, melodies that contain many skips tend to sound angular and to have a more instrumental character. Example 39 is an excerpt from a "partita" (suite) for solo violin by Bach. It consists primarily of skips, and produces an exciting melodic line that is certainly more suited for an instrument than a voice.

EXAMPLE 39

Most long melodies, in particular those composed by Mozart, maintain a balance between scale passages and skips. Example 40 contains the first 40 bars of the last movement of Mozart's 39th symphony. The passage can be divided into three sections of almost equal length. The first section (bars 1–15) is constructed of scales, the second (bars 16–27) of skips, and the last (bars 28–40) of both scales and skips. The result is a beautifully proportioned and highly pleasing melodic line.

EXAMPLE 40
Allegro

EXERCISE

Examine the opening passages of each movement of Mozart's *Eine Kleine Nachtmusik* to see how skips alternate with scale runs. (Workbook, Section IV, Exercise 7)

The character of a melody will not only be affected by the predominance of either steps or skips in general, but it will also be affected by the presence of certain specific intervals. Any interval reappearing a number of times will tend to dominate the character of a melody. The continued use of 3rds and 6ths, for example, will invariably produce a warm, lyric sound.

EXAMPLE 41

On the other hand, 4ths and 5ths are strong intervals, and will remain so even within lyric or chromatic passages. A well-known theme from Wagner's *Tristan und Isolde* affords a particularly good example of this.

EXAMPLE 42

The larger the intervals become, the more expressive they tend to sound. Example 43, also from *Tristan und Isolde,* achieves its emotional character from the use of minor 7ths coupled with scale passages.

In writing atonal music, where there is no key center, composers tend to exploit the effect of specific intervals, and to

use them in unusual ways. The short theme from Alban Berg's
Lyric Suite contains all the intervals arranged in order from a
2nd to a 7th. (Example 44.)

EXAMPLE 43

EXAMPLE 44

An excessive use of large, dissonant intervals, particularly
major 7ths and minor 9ths, invariably produces highly intense,
erratic line. At the same time, a considerable degree of excite-
ment can be generated, as in the beginning of a song by Anton
Webern. (Example 45.)

EXAMPLE 45

Examine the passages suggested below and note the types of intervals they contain, and the manner in which these intervals affect the character of the melodies.

1. In the English horn solo at the beginning of the third act of Wagner's *Tristan und Isolde,* a particularly melancholy effect is produced by the appearance of a number of perfect 4ths and 5ths, which are then altered at calculated moments to become augmented and diminished. (Workbook, Section IV, Exercise 8)

2. In the opening bars of the prelude to Wagner's *Die Meistersinger,* a strong majestic effect is produced by a combination of diatonic scale passages with perfect 4ths. (Workbook, Section IV, Exercise 9)

The most important exercises for this chapter are those affecting ear training. Be able to hear and sing every interval in example 36 both ascending and descending. The fastest way to identify these intervals is to find a variety of familiar melodies that begin with each of these skips. For example, the opening theme of Beethoven's *Eroica* symphony begins with an ascending major 3rd, the opening of the Fifth symphony with a descending major 3rd, the *Star Spangled Banner* with a descending minor 3rd, etc.

It is not enough to be able to master the intellectual content of this chapter. A musical experience must ultimately depend on a person's reaction *to what he hears*. Remember, the ear is not an absolute entity; it can always be trained to hear more critically and perceptively.

Define:
　　Interval
　　Melodic inversion
　　Major interval
　　Minor interval
　　Perfect interval
　　Imperfect interval
　　Augmented interval
　　Diminished interval

7

TRIADS—RELATIONSHIPS BETWEEN THREE NOTES

IN THE PREVIOUS CHAPTER, we noted that certain types of intervals can be constructed from notes of the major scale, but that others must make use of chromatic tones. We have seen the effect of these intervals on a variety of melodies, some highly chromatic, a few atonal. This book will remain, however, a study of diatonic music, and occasional observations made beyond this sphere will merely serve to place this specific style within its proper position among the numerous styles of Western music.

The characteristic qualities of the various intervals are so closely related to the very nature of musical sound itself that they will remain constant to some extent both within and without a central tonality. This statement does not hold true of combinations of three or more notes. Here, the key center definitely limits the pitches that can be sounded together. The student who found the minute categories of two-note intervals confusing might well have been appalled at the thought of examining all the possible combinations of three notes. In one sense, however, the material becomes simpler the more notes are sounded together. In order for music to remain tonal, i.e., to remain within the limits imposed by a key center, only certain combinations of notes can be used.

The Four Types of Triads

The one interval most preferred for its harmonic possibilities during the eighteenth and nineteenth centuries was the 3rd. As a result, while intervals can consist of any combination of two notes, tonal chords are constructed *exclusively from* 3rds. A chord is by definition a combination of three or more notes.

Three-note combinations are called *triads*. Chords are built by placing thirds on top of each other. A third up from C is E, and a 3rd up from E is G. The combination of both these thirds produces C-E-G, called a C chord or a C triad. The triad built on D is D-F-A, a combination of the two 3rds D-F and F-A. One could continue to place more 3rds on top of these notes, but the results would become rather complicated after a time.

In limiting our first experiments to triads that can be constructed within the major key, we simply take each note of the scale and build a chord on it. The seven notes thus produce seven triads, which are numbered according to their position in the scale.

EXAMPLE 46

Limiting ourselves to the notes of the diatonic major scale, we need use only two types of 3rds: the major and the minor form. In the first chord in example 46, the distance from

C to E is a major 3rd; that from E to G a minor 3rd. Thus, the I chord in the key of C consists of a major 3rd on the bottom and a minor 3rd on top. The outer notes from C to G will then form a perfect 5th.

Now let us look at the second chord, built on the note D. Here, the placement of the 3rds is different, as the bottom interval D-F is minor, while the upper interval F-A is major. The outer notes D-A once again form a perfect 5th.

The difference in tone quality between these two types of triads is most striking. Both contain a major and a minor 3rd, but in varying positions. The chord with the major 3rd on the bottom is called a major triad, while the one with the minor 3rd on the bottom is called a minor triad. These two chords can be pictured abstractly as if they were made of different-sized boxes placed on top of each other.

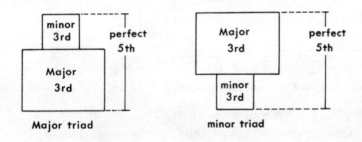

The student can now examine the triads built on the remaining notes of the scale, and identify those that are major and those that are minor. The chords built on C, F, and G will be found to be major, while those on D, E, and A will be minor. Only on B, the seventh note of the scale, will a situation appear in which two minor 3rds are placed on top of each other. This produces a new type of triad, one with a more dramatic, and less stable, sound. It is called a diminished triad, because the outer notes formed by the two 3rds B-D and D-F produce the interval of a diminished 5th B-F.

71

Having examined the triads that can be built on the C-major scale, let us note some general observations. Chords are built by superimposing 3rds on top of each other. In diatonic harmony, only major and minor 3rds appear. Four combinations of major and minor 3rds are therefore possible. These can be diagrammed as follows:

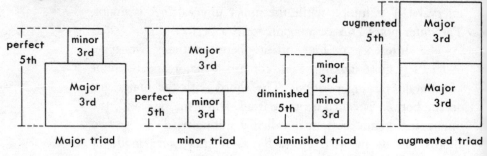

EXAMPLE 47

Major triad   minor triad   diminished triad   Augmented triad

The tone quality of each of these chords results from the intervals formed between the lowest note and the upper two notes. The lowest note is called the root, the next highest the 3rd, the upper note the 5th. In a major triad, the root will form a major 3rd and a perfect 5th with the upper notes. In a similar way, the minor triad will contain a minor 3rd and a perfect 5th, thus forming a somewhat darker sound. It is interesting to realize what considerable difference can be created merely by altering an E to an E♭, and changing a C-major to a C-minor chord.

The diminished triad will contain a minor 3rd and a diminished 5th between the root and the upper notes. The outer interval contributes significantly to the peculiar tension

72

of this chord. The last triad, the combination of two major 3rds, forms and augmented chord, thus named because of the augmented 5th appearing between the outer notes. This triad does not appear anywhere in the major diatonic scale.

The Triads Within the Major Scale

The particular color of any chord results from the intervals formed by the combinations of all the notes. The more stable the intervals, the more stable the triad will be. Diminished and augmented chords, with their imperfect 5ths, are highly colored and unstable. The augmented chord can be dismissed for the moment, since it does not appear in the major scale. Some attention must be paid to the diminished triad, however, for notwithstanding its unusual tone quality, it does appear on the seventh degree of the scale. The major and minor triads clearly supply the fundamental harmonic material, since they each appear in three different places. As the major triad is the more stable of the two chords, it follows that the three major triads found in the major scale will be the most important chords, and those most frequently used in tonal music.

In the key of C, the three major triads appear on C, F, and G, the first, fourth, and fifth degrees of the scale. This is rather interesting, since if we turn to the diagram of the circle of 5ths on p. 37 we will see that the F and G scales are most closely related to C. G lies a 5th above C, while F lies a 5th below. This balance gives these three chords their unique quality and relationship within the key of C. Built on the tonic, the C triad remains the center of harmonic focus. It is called the *tonic triad*. The G chord, built on the note a 5th above the tonic, is next in importance, and is called the *dominant* triad. We shall see how it plays a truly dominant role in tonal music. The F chord is built on a note a 5th below the tonic (actually the fourth degree of the scale), and is called the *subdominant* (literally, the underdominant). These three chords in their theoretical relationship to each other are shown in example 48. They contain all the notes of the major scale, and could conceivably be used exclusively throughout a composition.

EXAMPLE 48

After the three major triads, the minor triads occupy the next most important position. They can be found on the second, third, and sixth steps of the major scale, and derive their traditional names from their relationship to the major triads. Thus, the chord built on III, midway between I and V, is called the *mediant* triad (literally, the middle); the triad built on VI, the midpoint down from I (or VIII) to IV, is called the *submediant* (literally, under the middle). This leaves the II chord, directly above the tonic, which is called the *supertonic* (literally, above the tonic).

The VII chord a step below the tonic presents its own problems. Because it is different from the six other triads in ·that it is diminished, it is normally not given a separate name. Nor does it appear as frequently as the other triads. When it is used, it is treated in a special manner, to be discussed later. Since the seventh degree of the scale is called the leading tone because of its strong melodic tendency to lead to the tonic, the chord on VII is sometimes called the leading-tone triad.

Here then, in summary, are the common designations for all chords on the seven degrees of the major scale:

I. Tonic
II. Supertonic
III. Mediant
IV. Subdominant
V. Dominant
VI. Submediant
VII. Leading-tone triad

These terms should be memorized.

Triads and Their Relationship to Melodies

Even though a triad consists of only three notes, it can become a very exciting experience within a musical context. Often, a passage that sounds quite elaborate when played by a full orchestra will turn out on examination to be nothing more than a simple triad. The student must learn to recognize these passages by ear, and not to let his eye be fooled by the impressive look of the musical score. The triad maintains its identity no matter how the notes are arranged, or in what rhythm they appear.

In the last twenty-nine bars of Beethoven's Fifth Symphony (example 49), a heroic and triumphant effect is achieved through the constant repetition of one chord that maintains itself unqualified and unquestioned to the end of the composition.

Listen to the Prelude to Wagner's opera *Das Rheingold,* which contains the longest single triad in Western music. Harmonically, it consists of an E♭ chord sustained over 136 bars, although musically it is not at all dull. It begins with a single low note, the root, to which is added the 5th, and finally the 3rd. Gradually, more and more instruments enter as the

EXAMPLE 49

momentum increases right through to the end of the composition.

Let us examine some of the different positions in which a chord can appear, and note their different qualities. The three notes of the triad have been identified from the bottom up as the root, 3rd, and 5th. Now, the notes of a C-major chord can be so arranged that either C, E, or G will appear in the highest or lowest position. In the first three chords in example 50, the top voice changes; in the next three, the bottom note changes.

One point becomes immediately evident; alterations in the upper part do not change the sound of the chord as radically as do alterations in the lower part. If the succession of triads in example 50 is played slowly, the effect of the fifth chord, actually the first in which the bass moves, is quite startling, not to say unpleasant. A change in the position of a chord in which a note other than the root appears in the bass,

77

is called a harmonic inversion.[1] In the last two positions above, the triad appears in inversion. Certain inversions must be used carefully, and only under special circumstances. These will be discussed in more detail in Chapter 9. At present, the student should be aware of their existence, and be able to recognize a chord no matter how the notes are arranged. He should also be able to identify both major and minor triads with the root, 3rd, or 5th in the treble part. There are never any restrictions limiting changes in the upper position of a chord, as there are those limiting the use of inversions.

EXAMPLE 50

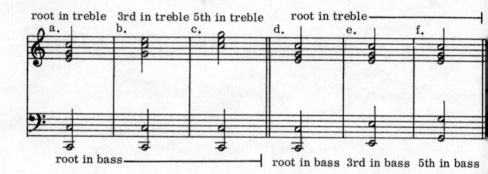

EXERCISE

Example 49 contains the C-major triad in root position (i.e., with the root in the bass) throughout. The student should be able to find the places where the root, 3rd, and 5th appear as the highest note.

Many melodies contain phrases based exclusively on the notes of a chord. For example, in the excerpt from Mozart's

---

[1] Note the similarity between the melodic inversion of an interval, and the harmonic inversion of a chord. In both cases, a note originally in an upper part is placed in the bass.

symphony quoted in example 40, the E♭-major triad can be found in bars 16-17 and 24-25, while the F-minor triad appears in bars 18-19 and 26-27. It is quite common for a composition to begin with a so-called "broken chord." [2]

How many of the following compositions in example 51 do you know? Can you identify all the chords?

EXAMPLE 51

---

[2] The technical name for a broken chord, i.e., a melodic succession of the notes of a triad, is an *arpeggio*.

Can you find 10 out of the 32 Piano Sonatas of Beethoven that begin with a broken chord in the melody line? How many Piano Sonatas of Mozart begin in this way? How many Preludes from the first book of Bach's *Well-Tempered Clavier?* (Workbook, Section V, Exercises 7–9)

These phrases represent the closest possible relationship between a melody and the harmony beneath it, since they both consist of the same notes. In the melody, they are played horizontally, as it were, and in the harmony vertically. This relationship can be symbolized by the single measure in example 52.

EXAMPLE 52

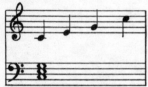

In actuality, however, in order for a melody to be harmonized with a C-major chord, it need not be confined to the notes C, E, and G. In our analyses of melodies in Chapter 3, we noted that tones could be introduced that were not normally a part of the scale. In a similar manner, a musical phrase sounding over a C-major triad can include tones other than those found in the harmony. The phrases in example 53 illustrate these possibilities.

In the first bar, the C-major chord is used to harmonize a phrase that consists of the same notes as the triad. In the second the melodic pattern is elaborated with two different passing notes. The chord tones harmonize with the underlying triad; the passing notes do not. For the fraction of a second that the notes D or F sound, a dissonance is created between that note and the chord. The extent of the dissonance can be determined by playing these notes as a unit, as in the third bar. The result is harmonically incomprehensible. If, however, the dissonance created by the note D is "resolved" by moving the note to a nearby chord tone, the passage becomes acceptable. Finally, in the last bar, the neighbor note appears over the C chord. The distance from the chord tone to the neighbor tone may be either a whole step or a half step, and the neighbor tone may or may not be a part of the scale.

EXAMPLE 53

Passing notes and neighboring notes increase the melodic interest in a composition. They also create a certain amount of tension, however momentary, between the melody and the accompaniment. The difficulty created for the student lies in the fact that, when he perceives notes in a passage other than those of the triad, he may not recognize their harmonic function (or lack of function, to be more specific). They do not affect the harmony at all, even though they greatly increase the scope of the melody. These *nonharmonic tones* may appear anywhere within the musical texture, at the top, bottom, or middle. More than one may appear at the same time. Example 54 is another passage from Beethoven's Fifth Symphony, one that occurs a few bars before example 49. Again, the harmony consists of nothing but a C-major chord for fifteen bars, but passing notes in the upper and lower parts greatly increase the harmonic interest. The passage is "reduced" from the full orchestral score, and is therefore not meant to be played on the piano, but it should be studied with recordings so that the effect of the passing tones can be perceived. Can you tell which of these non-harmonic tones are passing notes, and which are neighbor notes?

EXAMPLE 54

Admittedly, if nonharmonic tones appear too frequently, the expert as well as the student could have a difficult time determining which notes do and which notes do not belong to the underlying chords. In the last analysis, judgment must depend upon the ear itself. One should be able to hear which notes actually alter the harmony, and which merely appear for a moment, leaving the chords unchanged. It is quite conceivable that two people, both musically sensitive, could listen to the same passage, and arrive at different conclusions, both valid in their own way. Make sure that you *know* what you hear.

EXERCISE

Define:
Chord
Triad

Major triad
Diminished triad
Minor triad
Augmented triad
Tonic triad
Mediant
Dominant
Leading tone
Supertonic
Submediant
Harmonic inversion
Broken chord
Nonharmonic tone
Passing tone
Neighbor tone
Arpeggio

8

CHORD PROGRESSIONS

WE ARE NOW READY to examine the most important single subject in the entire study of tonal harmony: how chords move from one point to the next. The creation of a musical structure consists fundamentally of the invention of chord progressions, which are then expanded into elaborate proportions. We sometimes assume that the composer first invents a melody, and then harmonizes it. Nothing could be further from the truth. Composers most frequently conceive of chord sequences first, which then becomes elaborated or decorated into a melody. The melody is the upper voice of the harmony. In this chapter, we shall see how this process of composition takes shape.

Keyboard Harmony

In the last chapter, we learned how chords could be identified, and, to some extent, how they could be distinguished from surrounding nonharmonic tones. The three notes of a triad can be arranged in different ways, and can appear in different spatial positions. This maneuverability of the triad, especially in the treble register, allows the composer to move effortlessly from one chord to another, and to employ a considerable variety of choice in this movement.

Let us limit all chords at present to simple triads in root position. This means that when the exercises are played on the piano, the root of the chord will be played with the left hand, doubling the note in octaves if so desired; the right hand will play the complete triad in some position so that either the root, 3rd, or 5th will appear in the uppermost part. (Example 55.)

EXAMPLE 55

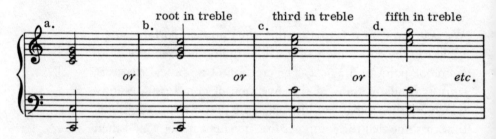

If a composer wanted to move from a C triad to an F triad, he would *not* follow one chord with the other as in example 56.

EXAMPLE 56

Rather, he would arrange the notes of the upper part, played by the right hand, in such a way that each of the three notes would move as smoothly as possible to the nearest scale degree for the next chord.

86

EXAMPLE 57

Right!

Let us imagine these passages played by an orchestra, with a separate instrument performing each part. In example 56, each voice would move up a 4th to the next. In example 57, however, the instrument playing the upper line would repeat the two Cs; that playing the next lower part would move up a major 2nd from G to A; the next part would move up a minor second from E to F, while the lowest part would move up a 4th, following the roots of the chords from C to F. Thus, of the four separate voice parts, one stays the same, while three move up. A final change which would make the pattern even more varied would be to raise the first note in the bass up an octave so that the lower part, still moving from C to F, would now descend a 5th instead of ascending a 4th. The final form of the progression is found in example 58.

EXAMPLE 58

A maximum of musical interest has been achieved in example 58. For now the bass moves down, the two middle voices move up, while the top voice stays the same. If the student compares this arrangement with that found in example 56, he will find that where each part merely jumped up a perfect 4th, no variety of movement, and only a minimal amount of musical interest resulted. As long as we can vary the triad by placing it in a number of different positions in the treble register, we can obtain more interest.

After considering the above examples, and the reasons why one would prefer a movement from a C chord to an F chord as it was done in example 58 rather than as in example 56, one can deduce a general procedure. This procedure is followed in all the music composed in the tonal period, and should be carefully observed by the student until it becomes an instinctive part of his musical thinking. If possible, do not move all the voice parts in the same direction at the same time. This type of movement, called *parallel motion,* is demonstrated in example 56. The progressions in example 57 are more acceptable; there, three voices move up, while one stays the same. This is called *oblique motion.* Most preferable, however, are those shown in example 58, where some voice parts move down, while others move up. This is called *contrary motion.*

EXERCISE

Practice playing the following two-chord progressions at the keyboard, all in contrary or oblique motion. Begin each progression with the root, then the 3rd, then the 5th, of the initial chord in the uppermost part. Write the progressions in half notes, as in the examples above. (1) G major to C major, A minor to D minor, D minor to G major, E minor to A minor. (2) C major to A minor, F major to D minor, A minor to F major, F minor to C major. (3) D major to G major, E major to A major, A minor to F♯ minor, D major to B minor. (4) B♭ major to G minor, G minor to E♭ major, G♭ major to E♭ minor, D♭ major to G♭ major.

Fundamental Chord Progressions

We have seen how chords can move most smoothly from one to the other. The next problem to consider is in what order the various chords should be placed. Why should one choose to follow a C chord by an F chord? Why not use an F♯ chord instead? Theoretically, any chord can precede or follow any other chord. Certain progressions, however, will obviously sound different from others. The student must learn to recognize the effect of these different progressions if he is to know which to use, and where to use them. In actual practice, a very limited number of progressions are preferred, while others are found only infrequently. Different types of progressions will traditionally appear in different parts of a composition.

Our first analysis of chord progressions will be confined to the six fundamental triads within any major key as they are constructed on the first six degrees of the scale. Remember that these consist of three major triads (on I, IV, and V) and three minor triads (on II, III, and VI). The triad on VII is diminished, and at least for now, outside the realm of our investigations.

Without a doubt, the most important two-chord progression used throughout the tonal period is that where the dominant chord (V) moves to the tonic (I). In practice, this is a method of approaching the tonic chord. Any progression that leads to the tonic tends to support and establish that chord as the central one in the key. This V-I progression, then, is invariably found near the beginnings of most compositions, and again at the end. It is so common for a piece of music written in the tonal period to end with a V-I cadence[1] that almost all other endings are considered exceptional, and remain comparatively

[1] A cadence is a melodic or a harmonic pattern indicating the end of a phrase, a passage, or an entire composition.

rare. Quite often in the works of Beethoven, this two-chord movement is repeated over and over again. Beethoven's Fifth Symphony affords a classic example of the procedure, and the last fifty-odd bars consist of nothing but tonic and dominant chords moving back and forth until finally nothing is left but the tonic chord. This, then, remains for the last twenty-nine bars (see example 47).

The acoustical principle functioning behind this V-I movement is contained within the circle of fifths. The key to the affirmative power of this progression apparently lies in the fact that the bass notes move down a 5th (or up a 4th). This would produce a clockwise step around the circle of fifths. It is necessary to learn to recognize by ear and to play on the piano V-I progressions in all positions and in all keys. In order to most benefit from practice, begin all progressions with the tonic chord. In that way it will always be known in what key they are being played. Thus, a three-chord progression I-V-I should be practiced in all keys, around the circle of fifths, as illustrated in example 59. If octaves cannot be played with the left hand, a single note will do as well.

EXAMPLE 59

In a very broad sense, a progression longer than three chords can often be seen to be an expansion of this fundamental movement. Most melodies consist of harmonic progressions to two separate chords as goals: the first progression moves from the tonic to the dominant, the second back again to the tonic.

This is neatly demonstrated in the beginning of a sonata by Mozart. (Example 60.)

EXAMPLE 60

On an even broader aspect, when one examines an entire movement of a sonata or a symphony, one usually finds the composition beginning in the tonic key, moving away from this to a section in the dominant key, and finally returning to the tonic at the end. The sonata movement above that began in D comes to a full stop in A 58 bars later, and moves back to close in D at bar 150.

EXAMPLE 61

Finally, on the broadest possible level, if one considers an entire sonata or symphony in three or four movements, the first and last movements will always be written in the tonic key, the middle movements in other keys. In this same sonata by Mozart, the middle movement is in the dominant key. (Example 62.)

EXAMPLE 62

Thus, a harmonic movement away from, and then back to, the tonic, appears not only as a structural building block for short harmonic progressions, but also as a miniature symbol for an entire musical composition.

Beginning, then, with this fundamental three-chord unit, we should consider how it can be expanded. From the forceful V-I progression we can isolate the idea of a root moving down a perfect 5th (or up a perfect 4th) and apply it in a number of places, still using the six fundamental triads within the major scale. Thus, if V tends to move down a 5th to I, then in a similar manner I can move down to IV, II to V, III to VI, and VI to II. These fragments can be combined together in numerous ways so that II can move to V and then to I, or even into a longer III-VI-II-V-I progression. Here, each chord moves down a 5th to the next, eventually culminating in the final V-I progression.

Of all the progressions based on this root movement, the ones most often found are those emphasizing the three major triads (I, IV, and V), since they tend to be more stable than the minor triads. As a result, the most common progressions found after V-I will be I-IV and II-V. These will frequently combine to make up longer sequences, such as I-IV-I, I-IV-V-I, I-II-V-I, and finally I-IV-II-V-I.

EXERCISE

Learn to play each of the four progressions above in all positions and in all keys, moving around the circle of fifths. Then, without looking at a piano, write out the progressions in keyboard style in selected keys. (Workbook, Section VI, Exercises 2–4)

At this point let us leave these abstract conceptions for a moment, and examine some music. Example 63 is a familiar passage from Brahms' First Symphony. First, identify each chord as it appears, taking into consideration every note that is actually *sounding* at any given moment (as in the second full bar, where the C is still sounding on the third beat). After

93

identifying each chord determine its position on the C scale, and write below the bass staff the Roman numbers as the chord changes. Note every progression where the root moves up a perfect 4th.

EXAMPLE 63

Allegro non troppo ma con brio

Keeping in mind the fact that the meaning of any progression is revealed in its ultimate goal, it is now possible to experiment with other types of chord movement. After the fundamental direction noted above, that where the root moves down a 5th, the next most common progression is one where the root moves down a 3rd. This usually appears as a three-chord sequence, for example I-VI-IV, where the I moves down a 3rd to VI, and the VI down a 3rd to IV. Thus, the original progression down a 5th I-IV has been expanded by the presence of an intervening chord.

This type of movement often takes the form I-VI-IV-II, ending V-I. The progression V-III-I does not appear too fre-

94

quently because the V chord tends to move directly to I. V-III-I then sounds as if the III has intruded itself between the outer chords.

Given these two methods of constructing strong chord progressions, one by moving the root down in 5ths, the other by moving it down in 3rds, they can be combined in a number of ways to construct longer progressions.

EXERCISE

Construct a chord progression moving from the tonic to the dominant (or to a V-I cadence), first by supplying one missing chord (I-?-V-I), then two (I-?-?-V-I), continuing up to five. Limit all chord movements to those in which the root moves either down a 5th or down a 3rd. First, write out the Roman numbers for the progression; then select the key; then play it at the piano. Next, write it out in keyboard style, and finally play it in all the major keys. (Workbook, Section VI, Exercise 6, 7)

The next general type of harmonic movement, in which the root moves either up a 3rd or up a 5th, is found less frequently in tonal music, although it is certainly not rare. The resulting sequences are sometimes called weak progressions, although the phrase is rather poor in that it suggests a negative evaluation. These progressions usually appear in limited circumstances. A strong progression moving down in 3rds can, for all practical purposes, continue indefinitely; and the composer can follow a movement from I to VI by one from VI to IV, then IV to II, etc. On the other hand, a progression moving up a 3rd will not immediately be followed by another moving up a 3rd. Thus, if one chord moves to the next with a "weak" progression, the movement of the second chord to the third should be such that *the over-all direction from the first to the third chord will form a strong progression.* For example, if I moves up to III, then III tends to move either to IV or to VI, forming a total movement from I to IV, or from I to VI, both strong progressions.

The same procedure holds true for chords moving up in 5th (or down in 4ths). When such a movement appears, it should be followed by a chord that will turn the entire harmonic direction into a strong one. If II moves down a 4th to VI, the VI will then most likely move to V, forming an over-all pattern from II to V. I-V-VI is also commonly found.

This leaves only one other possible type of harmonic movement: that in which the root moves up or down in 2nds. Those in which the root moves up a 2nd are more commonly found than those in which the root moves down a 2nd. This type of stepwise motion often appears as a "deceptive progression." A chord sounds as if it is going in one direction, but suddenly shifts to an unexpected goal for a moment. If the original progression involves a V-I movement, the V might first resolve up a second to VI, and then return to V to conclude with the proper V-I progression. In other words, the psychological effect of the progression I-V-VI-V-I is to postpone for a moment the proper resolution of the dominant to the tonic. (See example 64.)

EXAMPLE 64

C: I   V   VI   V   I

Progressions in which the root moves up a step have already been noted in such sequences as I-II-V-I, I-IV-V-I, and I-III-IV.

But rarely do two stepwise chords occur in direct succession, as for example I-II-III. The difficulty of stepwise progressions lies in the fact that they tend to produce similar motion in the voice parts. In a stepwise progression, the student should *always* employ contrary motion, if possible between the outer voices.

EXAMPLE 65

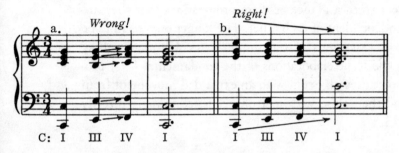

The student should familiarize himself with the sounds of these various progressions. He should be able to perform them on the piano in a simple block-chord style as outlined in example 65. He should be able to recognize them when he hears them played.

EXERCISE

The following progressions should be practiced at the piano in all keys, with the upper part of the chords in various positions.

1.   I-V-I

                 I-IV-I

                 I-IV-V-I

                 I-II-V-I

                 I-IV-II-V-I

2.   I-VI-V-I

                 I-VI-II-V-I

97

I-VI-IV-V-I
I-VI-IV-II-V-I

3.   I-III-IV-V-I
             I-III-VI-V-I
             I-III-VI-IV-V-I

It is clear from a glance at these progressions that they are
not at all independent of each other. The longer ones seem to be
variations or extensions of the shorter ones. Ultimately, they
can all be said to be elaborations of the fundamental I-V-I progression, since they all begin with an expanded movement from
I to V, and then close with a strong cadence moving directly
from V to I.

Chord Progressions and Melodic Construction

Anyone who prepares original assignments should follow
the same procedure a composer would use in creating a large
musical form. He should begin with a harmonic progression,
then place it in some rhythmic form, say one chord to a bar.
Finally, with his underlying structure fixed, he can invent a
melody to fit over the progression. Let us examine these three
steps in order to see how they can best be carried out.

The right hand should be kept free to play the melody.
Therefore, the harmony must be performed by the left hand
alone. As before, we do not want to move all the voices in parallel motion. Thus, if we wanted to progress from I to V, we
would *not* play the chords as shown in example 66.

Instead, we should break up the harmony, playing first the
bass note, and then the rest of the chord in a higher position.
Even though the chord appears *after* the bass, the ear will

hear the entire bar as a single harmonic unit, and will understand the first isolated note as the bass of the chord. We can thus
place the chord itself in any convenient position. The following,
example 67, would be a preferred way of playing the same I-V
progression as above.

EXAMPLE 66

Eb: I   V

EXAMPLE 67

or   etc.

Eb: I   V

If the melody were in $\frac{3}{4}$ time, then the bass note could be
a quarter note, and the chord a half note in the rhythm ♩♩ ,
or the reverse could be tried ♩♩ , with the chord not enter-
ing until the third beat in the bar. The chord could also be repeated in quarter notes, forming the pattern: note-chord-chord,
as in a waltz. Thus, we can obtain considerable rhythmic variety
with these simple spacings of the chords.

Now, we must plan a harmonic rhythm for the progression.
The harmonic rhythm indicates the frequency with which the
chord changes. Remember that tonal melodies tend to be
symmetrical in structure, with one phrase balanced by a second

of equal length. This produces an overall pattern of two bars plus two, or four plus four. The most significant difference in the harmony of these two phrases, one fundamental to the entire idea of tonality, is that the first half of the melody moves away from the tonic, and the second half moves back. At its simplest, the first phrase moves I-V, the second V-I. The underlying I-V-I progression then forms a miniature drama in which the tonic is first established, then abandoned for a new goal, and finally reaffirmed as the last chord. Example 68 shows the bass pattern for a simple melodic phrase.

EXAMPLE 68

A: I   V   V   I

Now, how does the melody derive from the chords? Of course, the tones of the chord can be used exclusively, and the notes C, E, and G used with the C-major triad, and G, B, and D for the G-major triad. Passing tones can also be employed, as in example 53. Some traditional rules of procedure, however, should be noted. Often, when the melody skips, particularly when the skip comes within the measure, the chord will not change; the underlying harmony should be applicable to both notes. (Example 69.)

On the other hand, if the melody remains on the same note, particularly if this note is repeated over the bar line, then the harmony should change. This will provide variety, and bring out the natural rhythmic accent at the beginning of each measure. (Example 70.)

EXAMPLE 69

EXAMPLE 70

Construct four- and eight-bar patterns of harmonic progressions, and then try to place melodies over them. Here is one hint. Eight-bar patterns often contain two four-bar patterns similar to each other except for their final goals. The first four bars can end on the dominant, the last four on the tonic. The following pattern could, with a little experimenting, produce profitable results: I-IV-V, I-V-I, or I-VI-IV-V, I-VI-V-I. Patterns can also be varied so that the chords will change twice in a bar, or one chord will be sustained for two bars. It is not recommended to try Wagner's device (used in the prelude to *Das Rheingold*) of sustaining the same triad for 136 bars! Try to invent your own harmonic patterns, and even try to vary the harmonic goals, perhaps aiming first for the supertonic, or subdominant, and then returning from there to the tonic.

Four-Part Harmony

This final method of arranging and spacing chords is most important, but rather diifficult to learn to control. It is called four-part, or four-voice, harmony. Tonal harmony, consisting fundamentally of three- and four-note chords, appears most often in a four-voiced texture. When the simple triads are arranged in piano style, as in earlier examples above, a three-note chord appears in the treble above a bass sometimes doubled in octaves. In four-part harmony, only four separate notes are sounded at one time, and no parts are doubled. The notes are evenly distributed throughout the treble and bass registers.

This texture grows out of the fundamental nature of tonal harmony, and has in turn produced a number of supporting musical sound structures. For example, a chorus or choir usually consists of four parts: soprano, alto, tenor, and bass. The most preferred form of chamber music is the string quartet, consisting of two violins, a viola, and a cello. Even in a full symphony orchestra, each instrumental family contains four fundamental parts. The strings consist of violins, violas, cellos, and double basses; the wood winds consist of flutes, oboes, clarinets, and bassoons; and the brass winds of trumpets, french horns, trombones, and tubas. Other instruments, such as piccolos (which are actually high flutes), bass clarinets, etc., are usually considered additional. A great deal of keyboard music can also be seen to be simply four-part music. Thus, when we speak of "four voices" in part music, we do not necessarily refer to human voices. This word can be applied to instrumental music as well. The separate parts are invariably referred to as the soprano, alto, tenor, and bass, even though they may be played by separate instruments, or even reproduced on a single instrument, as in a keyboard fugue by Bach. Thus, in the family of stringed instruments, the violin is the soprano, the viola the alto, and the cello the tenor. The double basses, needless to say, are the basses!

The problem of composing music for four independent voices is considerable. For the present, we will only practice arranging simple chord progressions for four voices. The composer must first try to keep each part within the range appropriate for that voice. He must also, to the extent that he is able, write for each part a singable line, or at least one that is to some degree interesting. The normal ranges for the four singing voices are shown in example 71a.

An octave and a fifth is a fairly safe limit for a choral voice, although most trained solo singers can usually control a two-octave range. Individual instruments often have even larger ranges. (See example 71b.)

Insofar as the individual voice parts are considered as separate units, it can hardly be expected for one to write perfect counterpoint, with four equally beautiful melodies proceeding simultaneously in perfect harmony, very easily. At present, it

EXAMPLE 71

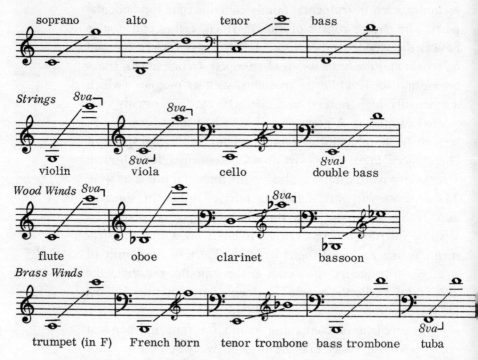

will suffice to utilize the following two simple rules: 1. Keep each part moving smoothly, and avoid too many consecutive jumps. 2. Do not keep any part moving over the same two or three-note area for any period of time.

Up to this point, many harmonic patterns have been practiced at the piano. Four-part patterns, however, must be written in an evenly spaced pattern in which two voices appear in the treble range, and two in the bass. (See example 72.)

This step toward equal balance can often be achieved by arranging the upper three parts in what is called open position. In open position, a chord is spaced in such a way that its three tones are not placed directly together on the staff.

One traditionally never allows more than an octave to intervene between any two adjacent voices except between the tenor

and bass. There, a distance of more than an octave is always
acceptable.

EXAMPLE 72

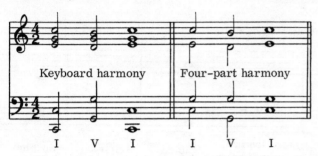

EXAMPLE 73

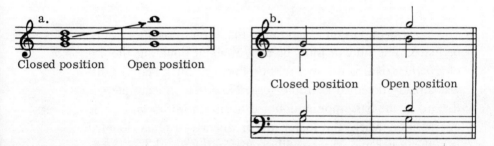

In arranging a chord for four voices, the root, at least for
the present, should appear in the bass. Nevertheless, if four
voices are to be sounding a three-note chord, then one note of
the chord must always appear in two different places. In other
words, either the root, 3rd, or 5th must be doubled. Some experimenting with different possibilities, which the student
should try, will reveal the following points: 1. The root can
always be doubled in any position. 2. For variety, and for the
sake of the individual voice parts, the 3rd or 5th may be doubled
instead, except in one instance to be noted below. 3. On occa-
sions, the 5th may be omitted, and the resulting chord may
contain two roots and two 3rds, or even three roots and one

3rd. On no account can the root be eliminated from a triad, as one could not then identify the chord, or the 3rd, as this would result in an open 5th, an ambiguous harmonic interval within the tonal system. (See example 74.)

EXAMPLE 74

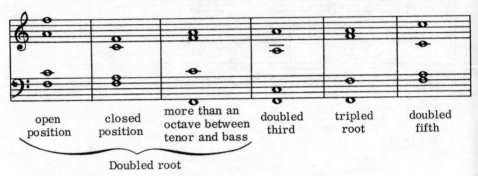

| open position | closed position | more than an octave between tenor and bass | doubled third | tripled root | doubled fifth |

Doubled root

One very important exception to the second rule above must be noted. The student must be careful about doubling the 3rd of a *major* triad, as it sometimes produces a "thick" effect (this was already noted in example 50e). Note that in example 50e the 3rd in the bass appears doubled in the chord above it. The one position where the major 3rd frequently appears doubled is in the upper two voices, as illustrated in the fourth bar above.

Here, then, in conclusion, is a I-II-V-I progression in two different versions (example 75), the first in keyboard style, the second in four parts.

EXAMPLE 75
a. Keyboard harmony

b. Four-part harmony

Note that all the chords in the four-part version appear in open position. Note also the doubled third in the II chord, a minor triad. One other significant aspect of this texture should be noted. The sound is so carefully spaced that any two of the four voices can be played together satisfactorily.

Although a triad remains incomplete without all three notes, the sequence of intervals created by the combination of any two voice parts above remains satisfactory. Even the open octaves and the 5ths sound acceptable within their context. Let us consider only the alto and tenor voices. (Example 76.)

EXAMPLE 76

The four intervals formed are, in order: a 6th, an octave, a 5th, and a 6th. The "harmonious" effect of the first and final 6th appears vividly in contrast to the colder sound of the octave and 5th. Always keeping in mind this difference between the sound quality of the intervals, never allow the octave or 5th to become too prominent. One must, therefore, never create a situation in which any two voices within a four-part texture form two 5ths or two octaves in succession. To note the effect

of this procedure, let us examine another version of the I-II-V-I
progression with a different spacing. (Example 77.)

EXAMPLE 77

First play the bass and alto part alone. They will form the
consecutive intervals of a 3rd, 3rd, octave, and 5th. The octave
followed by the 5th is perfectly acceptable here. Now, try the
soprano part with that of the tenor (5th, 5th, 6th, 6th). The
first two 5ths together sound so odd and hollow that even the
6ths following them cannot make the passage sound even
remotely agreeable.

Therefore, in order to insure the most harmonious four-
part music possible, one should bear in mind the following
rules:

TO SPACE A SINGLE CHORD

1. In choosing a note of a triad to be doubled, use the root
where possible. The 5th can also be doubled, as can the 3rd of
a minor triad. Doubling the 3rd of a major triad, especially in
the lower voices, sometimes produces unsatisfactory results.

2. Keep the greatest distances between the two lower parts,
and the least space between the three upper parts. Do not allow
more than an octave to appear between the soprano and alto, or
between the alto and tenor (this rule is sometimes broken by

composers in order to assure a more interesting melodic line).

To Move from One Chord to Another

1. Consecutive 3rds and 6ths can appear between any two voice parts, but perfect 5ths and octaves should proceed to different intervals within the same two voices. Never allow consecutive 5ths or octaves to appear between any two notes of the same voice parts.[2]

2. Keep the four voices moving in contrary or oblique motion at all times. Never move all the voices in the same direction at the same time.

EXERCISE

Arrange each of the chord progressions on pages 97–98 in a different key, and in a four-part form. Begin one progression with the root of the first chord in the soprano, the next with the 3rd in the soprano, and the next with the 5th. (Workbook, Section VI, Exercise 10)
Identify the following terms:

Keyboard harmony
Four-part harmony
Parallel motion
Oblique motion
Contrary motion
Parallel 5ths

[2] Another rule often added by theorists asks the student never to approach a perfect interval between any two voices with parallel motion. In other words, two voices coming together to form a perfect interval should approach it with either oblique or contrasting motion.

Parallel octaves
Harmonic rhythm
Open position
Closed position
Cadence
Deceptive progression
Strong progression
Weak progression

PART III

*Elaboration of the
Fundamental Materials*

9

INVERSIONS OF CHORDS

PARTS I AND II of this book presented the principal aspects of harmonic movement as practiced during the tonal period. The fundamental material has been seen to consist of scales and triads. The structure of tonality has been revealed in the laws governing the chord sequences. These sequences were controlled by the movements of the roots of the triads.

Now, in Part III, a series of traditional elaborations or expansions of this material will be presented. These elaborations supply variety and contrast within the harmonic order set up in the Parts I and II. For example, inversions (this chapter) permit the chords to take on new positions through the placing of notes in the bass other than the root; nonharmonic tones (Chapter 10) add to the richness of the general vocabulary by allowing pitches to appear that are not part of the chords at all; the minor scale (Chapter 11) alters the makeup of almost every chord; and finally, 7th and 9th chords (Chapter 12) permit extra notes to be added to the triad above the root.

Before a study of these next chapters is undertaken, it should be noted that the fundamental procedures outlined in the previous chapters *never change*. No matter how chords are altered, no matter what note appears in the bass, no matter what nonharmonic tones sound with the chord, *the principles of root movement do not change.* The root may not appear in the bass; in fact, it may conceivably not even appear in the chord. Nevertheless, the rules governing the progression from one goal to the next remain the same.

The Principle of Overtones

In considering the possible ways to space a chord, it was noted in Chapter 8 that the higher in the register one moved, the more closely together the notes could be placed. On the other hand, the lower in the register the notes appeared, the farther apart they had to be placed. This observation was formulated in the rule that one should never allow a distance of more than an octave to appear between any adjacent upper voices in a four-part chord, while one could allow more than an octave between the tenor and bass. Too many notes placed too low in the register tend to sound muddy and unclear. Compare, for example, the difference in the sound of these two spacings of the interval of a 6th as shown in example 78.

EXAMPLE 78

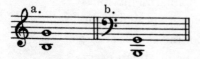

The version in the bass has none of the mellowness or sweetness one normally associates with this interval. If anything, it sounds slightly dissonant. The reasons for this will soon become apparent.

When a sound is created, let us say by the vibrations of a string, the entire length of the string moves back and forth at a specific number of vibrations per second.

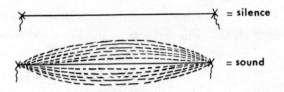

As we already know, the faster the string vibrates, the higher the pitch sounds. Surprisingly, at the same time that the string is vibrating as a complete unit, it is also divided in half, each half vibrating twice as fast as the entire string.

This produces an interesting result. The single string is actually sounding more than one pitch at the same time. The one heard most strongly, of course, is that produced by the entire string, but the one an octave higher is also heard at the same time, although less audibly. In actuality, the string vibrates not only as an entire unit, and not only in halves, but also in thirds, in fourths, etc., producing a series of pitches, each one higher and softer than the last. They are called overtones, or sometimes harmonics or partials. The first eleven overtones sounding from a low C are shown in example 79.

EXAMPLE 79

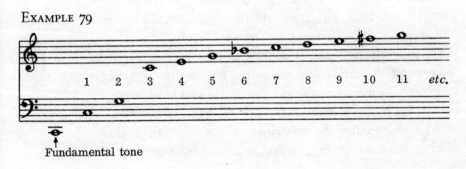

Fundamental tone

Because the notes of the piano are tuned in a "well-tempered" relationship, which allows us to perform in any key we choose, the pitches on the keyboard do not exactly coincide with those produced by the overtones of a given note. Consequently, the Bb and the F♯ above should be slightly lower.

It is this collection of overtones, the so-called high frequencies, that give to the low notes their full, rich sounds. Higher tones sound smaller and thinner because their overtones are less discernible. They quickly reach beyond the audible range of the human ear.

An examination of the overtones reveals some interesting facts. It actually explains to some extent why certain intervals sound more stable than others, and why the major triad holds such a fundamental position within tonal music. Let us first note that each new pitch in the series forms a different interval with its preceding note. Thus, reading from the bottom up, we find first an octave, then a perfect 5th, a perfect 4th, a major 3rd, a minor 3rd, a smaller minor 3rd (because the Bb should be slightly lower), a large major 2nd, two more normal major 2nds, a small major 2nd (because the F♯ should be slightly lower), and finally a minor 2nd.

Note that the three lowest intervals are all perfect: the octave, the 5th, and the 4th. This explains why they produce such a stable sound; they are the strongest and most audible of the overtones.

One final point to note is that the first five overtones form a major triad. Thus, we can see why the triad is the fundamental building block for tonal music. The solidity of this sonority is heard most clearly when it appears in root position with the intervals of the octave and 5th at the bottom. In using these spacings, one merely reinforces the overtones of the bass note itself. (See example 80.)

Thus, we see that the major triad is not a man-made invention; it is not an artistic creation produced by a sophisticated musical mind. Rather, it exists as a part of nature itself. That the major triad consists of the fundamental overtones of the initial note perhaps explain why it is traditionally supposed to sound "happy," while the minor triad is supposed to sound "sad." The minor triad is undoubtedly more unstable than the major, since it alters the fourth overtone changing the E♮ to E♭. If we keep the notes of the minor triad in the same position as those of the major triad above, we know acoustically and scientifically that along with the E♭, the E♮ is sounding at the very same time (although much softer, of course) as a part of the overtones of the bass note. This would certainly help create a darker tone color for this triad. (Example 81.)

EXAMPLE 80

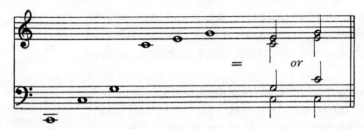

EXAMPLE 81

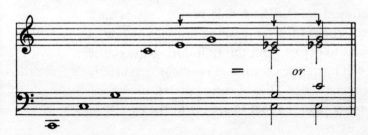

Diminished and augmented triads are even more unstable because they alter one of the fundamental intervals of the overtones: the perfect 5th itself. One can now see why the minor 6th in example 78b should sound so dissonant. Both notes set up entirely different overtones, which clash with each other in the upper registers.

EXERCISE

Reconstruct the overtones of these two notes to see exactly what sounds they produce. (Workbook, Section VII, Exercise 1)

Even with this scientific substantiation of the major triad, however, one cannot base all analyses of Western music on this premise. There is certainly no reason for creative art to follow natural law if it does not choose to. The courage and foresight that enabled great composers to utilize a norm when needed, but to depart from tradition when this was needed, certainly contributed to their *creative* stature. The major triad remains a natural phenomenon, but it is not in itself a work of art.

The fundamental principle of tonality, in which one establishes a key, then introduces "antitonic" elements, and finally overcomes them, combines in an ideal sense natural and artificial elements. The tonic triad in root position remains the fundamental acoustical unit of harmonic music, and as such the inevitable final chord of a composition. Since, however, a composer may want to depart from this unit during the course of the music, he will introduce chords and positions not directly related to the overtone series. One of these devices, inversions, allows for notes other than the root to appear in the bass.

First Inversion

The use of inversions aids the composer and arranger in a number of different ways. First, it provides a choice of different colorings for the same chord; second, it allows for a more flowing lyric line in the bass; finally, in the case of the tonic chord, it provides for the possibility of a semicadence or a half-cadence at the ends of phrases.

When the 3rd of a chord appears in the bass, the triad is said to be in the first inversion; when the 5th appears in the bass, it is said to be in the second inversion, regardless of whether the chord is major, minor, diminished, or augmented. (Example 82.)

EXAMPLE 82

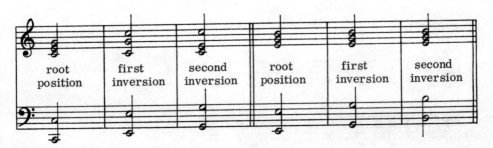

| root position | first inversion | second inversion | root position | first inversion | second inversion |

A first inversion can appear at any time, and be used as often as possible. It provides a welcome relief from the rigid accentuation of an endless series of triads in root position. One precaution must be taken, however. In the first inversion of a major triad, with the 3rd of the triad appearing in the bass, that note should not be doubled in any of the upper parts. If, in a C-major triad, the E appears in the bass, then it generates its own overtones, the strongest of which are B and G#. These clash with the C and G above, and thus should not be strengthened by the doubling of the E in an upper voice. It is better in this case to have the three upper parts contain two roots and a 5th. (See example 83.)

EXAMPLE 83

Wrong!   *Right!*

The minor triad, on the other hand, can appear in its first inversion without any restriction as to doubling. In fact, it often appears with the bass doubled in an upper voice. (See example 84.)

EXAMPLE 84

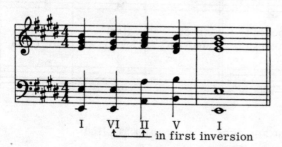

I   VI   II   V   I
in first inversion

Let us note the effect of different triads as they appear in first inversion. The special advantage of the tonic chord lies in the fact that it can be used this way without ending the flow of the music. Whenever a V-I progression appears, even in the middle of a composition, it tends to bring the music to a momentary halt. If, however, the dominant moves to a tonic chord that is not in root position, the feeling of finality is avoided, as this chord will in turn want to move to a farther resting point. At the very end of the composition, however, we would never want the tonic chord to appear with any other note but the root in the bass. (Example 85.)

EXAMPLE 85

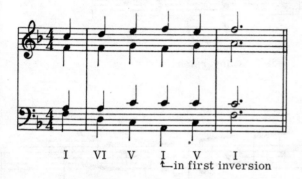

I   VI   V   I   V   I
              └─in first inversion

The II chord in first inversion is found very frequently at a cadence, where it tends to move to V. In fact, in the cadential pattern II-V-I, the II chord is most often found in the first inversion. Compare the two passages in example 86.

The III chord in the first inversion with the dominant of the key in the bass, takes on some of the characteristics of the dominant chord, and tends to move to the tonic. The III chord in root position tends to move either to VI or IV. (Example 87.)

EXAMPLE 86

I   V   I   II   V   I
              └in root position

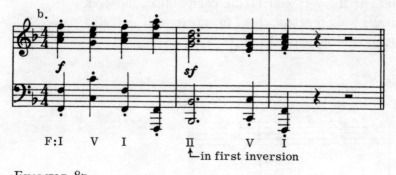

F:I   V   I   II   V   I

└─in first inversion

EXAMPLE 87

G: I   III   IV   III   I

└─in first inversion

The IV chord in the first inversion most frequently appears in the deceptive cadence V-IV. When V, instead of moving to I, moves somewhat unexpectedly to either IV or VI, the IV normally appears in first inversion. (Example 88.)

EXAMPLE 88

D: I   V   IV   V   I

└─in first inversion

There are no general restrictions on the use of either V or VI in the first inversion, other than the fact of V as a major chord. The bass note, B in the key of C, must therefore not be doubled in an upper voice, especially because it is the leading tone, and will most often move to the tonic. If two voices move simultaneously from B to C, consecutive octaves will result.

The possibility of a first inversion is most important in the VII chord, since this is the one position in which the chord normally appears. Since the leading-tone triad is diminished, it contains the interval of a diminished 5th between the root and the 5th (B-F in the key of C). If the triad were to appear in root position, the strongest overtone from B would be the *perfect* 5th F♯, which would clash with the F♮ of the chord. Similarly if the chord were to appear in the second inversion, with the F in the bass, then the strongest overtone would be *its* perfect 5th C. This would hardly improve matters, since the C would clash with the root B. Only when the diminished triad appears in the first inversion will the overtones not conflict, and the chord sound acceptable. The VII chord invariably acts in the same manner as a dominant and most often moves to I. In fact, VII often substitutes for the dominant chord. (See example 89.)

EXAMPLE 89

I   IV   I   VII   I
in first inversion

In addition to using this triad in the first inversion, be particularly careful about the voice leading. Whenever it appears, the B, the leading tone, tends to move to C. At the same time, the F, the diminished 5th, tends to move in the opposite direction, down a half step to E. The radical instability of the interval of the diminished 5th produces a situation where both notes must move to resolve the tension. The notes of this interval resolve by moving in half steps (see example 90), one up and the other down, to form the more consonant interval of the major 3rd.

EXAMPLE 90

Second Inversion

In experimenting with various notes of a chord to be placed in the bass, one soon realizes that the farther away one moves from the root, the less stable the result will sound. Thus, first inversions of major and minor triads can appear as often as the composer wishes, while second inversions are more restricted in their use. A second inversion, particularly of a major triad, has such a strong sound that it invariably calls attention to itself. This is not always desirable, and so this chord will tend to appear in limited circumstances.

As far as the spacing of the individual notes is concerned, there are no specific restrictions, and the bass may be doubled without ill effects. (See example 91.)

It is most important *never to approach this chord through a leap in the bass.* The bass notes both preceding and following a second inversion chord should be either identical with that of

the chord, or should move toward and from it in a stepwise
motion, as shown in example 92.

EXAMPLE 91

EXAMPLE 92

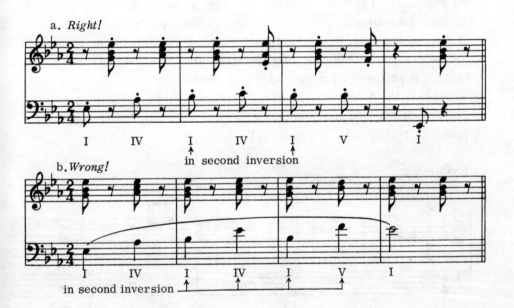

Only if the chord does not change can the bass part jump to
any pitch. In this context, the ear accepts the leap to the 5th in
the lowest part because the harmony remains the same. (Example 93.)

EXAMPLE 93

└ in second
 inversion

When the chords change, however, the bass note should never jump to or from a second-inversion chord.

In general, second inversions will not appear frequently in a composition. There is one place, however, where its appearance is quite common, and this is the final cadence. In the study of first inversions, we noted that the traditional V-I ending often followed a II chord in the first inversion. Just as often, the cadence is preceded by a tonic chord in the second inversion. This places the dominant note in the bass before the dominant chord itself appears, and produces a particularly strong anticipation of this chord. (Example 94).

EXAMPLE 94

I
∧ in second
└ inversion   V   I

Just as often, these two antepenultimate (next-to-next-to-last) chords—the II in the first inversion and the I in the second inversion—will combine to produce a cadence that is one of the harmonic clichés of the tonal period. There was surely no composer of the eighteenth and nineteenth centuries who did not avail himself of this progression. There the power of harmonic movement lies in the strong bass ascent from the subdominant to the dominant notes, balanced by the descent from the dominant to the tonic at the end.

EXAMPLE 95

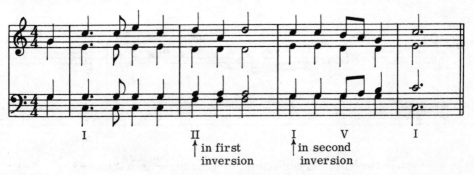

The effect of the tonic triad in the second inversion leading into the penultimate dominant is very striking, and was often used by composers of the eighteenth century. One frequently finds in the music of this period a fermata (a hold: ⌢) placed over this chord as an indication that the performer was to improvise a short cadenza at this point, postponing the dominant chord for a moment as shown in example 96.

EXAMPLE 96

b. As it might have been *performed.*

Even in the lengthier compositions of the nineteenth century, similar passages can be found. The long-held tonic chord in the second inversion continued to appear near the end of a concerto movement. At this point, the orchestra would stop, while the soloist would continue without accompaniment, performing or improvising a passage of considerable length. Eventually, when this cadenza was completed, the orchestra would re-enter, and the V-I cadence would complete the harmonic sequence. (See example 97.)

This example clearly shows how a harmonic progression can supply the structure for a lengthy symphonic movement. If the student were to hear a portion of a concerto movement, starting somewhere in the middle, and were to spot the sound of a long-held tonic chord in the second inversion, he would know he was near the end of the movement, and that the solo instrument was about to perform the cadenza. He would also know the movement would end with the return of the orchestra and the completion of the cadential progression.

EXAMPLE 97

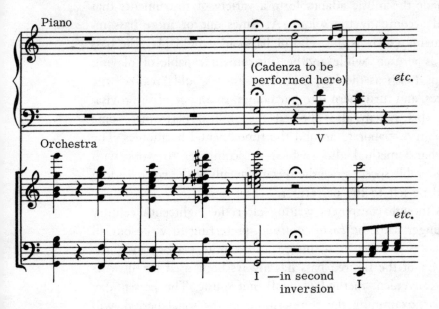

Figured Bass

The evolution of tonality, and of the rules governing the formation of chords, took many centuries. As a matter of fact, composers, who usually let their ears be their guide, wrote music consisting of what we today would call chords in root position long before any codified tonal system was established. It was not until the beginning of the seventeenth century that theorists came to realize that chords were conceived acoustically from the bass up. At this time, they developed a system of notational shorthand known as *basso continuo,* or figured bass, that was to be used from the seventeenth through the middle of the eighteenth century. The composer, writing a piece of music for voice or solo instrument with simple accompaniment, instead of completing the accompanying part, wrote only the bass line, and under it a series of numbers indicating the exact chords to be used. This system had certain distinct advantages. It made the music adaptable to a variety of instruments that could accompany the soloist. At times one or more bass instruments (such as the cello or bassoon) would play the bass line as written, while another instrument capable of playing chords (such as the harpsichord or lute) would "realize" the figures, and turn them into harmonies. In an age of improvisation, this system also allowed the skillful performer some freedom to elaborate around the fundamental harmonies. The shorthand method also enabled the composer to work with considerable speed, since the specific details of the voice leading could be left to the performer.

Although composers writing after the eighteenth century no longer used the *basso continuo,* preferring to write out all the notes themselves to insure an accurate performance, the concept of the figured bass has always been used by theorists as a convenient method of analyzing music. The present-day scholar, examining the compositions of the tonal period, will usually identify the chords and progressions by placing the proper figures below the bass line of his score. Traditionally, Roman numbers reveal the root of the chord in relationship to the tonic: Any form of a G chord within the key of F will be noted as II. On the other hand, the relationship of the individual chord to the note in the bass is indicated by Arabic numerals.

The system is fundamentally very simple. The figures represent the intervals between the written bass part and the notes forming the rest of the chord. Thus, a $\frac{5}{3}$ placed below a C would indicate the C-major triad in root position: 3 stands for the 3rd above the written C, i.e., E, while 5 stands for the 5th, G. If the key signature contained an E♭, then the numbers $\frac{5}{3}$ would indicate a C-minor chord, the 3 indicating a 3rd up from the bass note *within the scale* indicated by the key signature.

Now, suppose a composer wanted to notate a C triad in the first inversion, i.e., with the E in the bass. He would write the E, and then count the intervals between this note and the two other notes of the chord. Between the low E and the C above there would be a 6th; between the E and the G above there would be a 3rd. Thus, the first inversion would be indicated $^6_3$. Similarly, the second inversion, a C chord with a G in the bass, would be written $^6_4$, since the 6th above G would be E, and the 4th above C.

This, then, in principle, is the theory of the figured bass. In practice, however, composers tended to simplify so as not to write more than was absolutely necessary for the performer to comprehend the harmony. Thus, in a manner similar to secretarial shorthand, or to the Hebrew language (where the vowels are omitted if the words can be understood without them), some of the intervals are omitted from the notation. The first simplification applies to the triad in the root position, where no numbers are placed under the bass note. If one should find a G without any numerical indications, one would assume the chord to be in root position, and would play the G triad above it.

The second simplification concerns the 3rd above the bass. This is always understood to be sounded, and its indication is therefore omitted. Thus, a first-inversion triad is written simply 6, rather than $^6_3$. The $^6_4$ notation for the second inversion, on the other hand, remains unchanged.

The general rules for figuring simple chords are as follows: the root position triad contains no figures; the first inversion is indicated by a 6 placed below the bass note, the second inversion by $^6_4$.

What if a composer were to alter his chord, so that a C-major triad became augmented, i.e., C-E-G♯? Then, under the written C he would write ♯5, indicating that the 5th above the bass was to be raised a half step.

If, however, he wanted a C-minor chord, and the key signature did not include an E♭, he might simply place a ♭3 under the C. But the shorthand simplification eliminates the indication of the 3rd, so the composer merely writes the flat sign by itself. The rule can perhaps most clearly be stated in reverse order: if you wish to alter the notes of a chord, you must identify the interval of the pitch above the bass, and place the sharp, flat, or natural to the left of the number. The accidental appearing alone will always refer to the 3rd above the bass.

Let us suppose a composer wishes to write a C♯-minor triad (C♯-E-G♯) and there are no sharps or flats in the key signature. In root position, he would notate the C♯, and under it ♯5 (the 3rd, E, being understood). If the chord were to appear in the first inversion, he would notate the E, and below it write ♯6♯, the upper figure producing C♯, the lower G♯. If the second inversion was to be indicated, the composer would write the G♯, and below it 6♯4

The various figures for the major and minor triads, and their implied chords are shown in example 98. Be sure you understand *all* these constructions.

EXAMPLE 98

Implied chord

As succeeding chapters introduce new elaborations of the fundamental chords, the proper indications for the figured bass will be explained in each case. The figures for inversions of triads are so widely used that the student will often come across references, not to a first inversion, but to "a six chord," and not to a second inversion, but to "a six-four chord." The triad introducing the cadenza in the Classical concerto is, therefore, a tonic six-four chord.

EXERCISE

Identify the following terms:
Inversion
First inversion
Second Inversion
Overtones
Figured bass
Six chord
Six-four chord
Cadenza
Basso continuo

10

NONHARMONIC TONES

NEAR the end of Chapter 7 mention was first made of non-harmonic tones. These are notes appearing within a musical passage that cannot be analyzed as part of the underlying harmony. Since the colorful possibilities afforded by the use of these tones are quite rich and varied, it would seem advisable to consider the subject as a separate unit.

In general, one can observe that the continual use of non-harmonic tones increases the tension of the music through the momentary dissonances that appear between these notes and the harmony. Since dissonances must be resolved, they tend to increase the forward drive of the music. Finally, the melodic possibilities of the individual voice parts are considerably expanded.

One of the biggest problems facing anyone attempting to analyze a work such as Bach chorale would be to distinguish between notes that belong to the harmony and those that are foreign to it. In actuality, there are only a limited number of ways in which nonharmonic tones are normally used. These can be codified, then examined with comparative ease.

Passing Notes

Some simple types of nonharmonic tones have already been identified. One of these is the passing note (see example

53), which appears when a melody moves in steps along the scale. The passing note sounds between two other tones that form a part of the harmony.

EXAMPLE 99

In example 99a, the nonharmonic tone F appears as part of the scale pattern E-F-G. The outer notes E and G form a part of the underlying C-major chord. In 99b, the nonharmonic tone is altered to F♯, which is not a part of the C-major scale. In 99c, the passage has been expanded to include two passing notes, F and F♯, but this does not render the phrase any less comprehensible musically. In 99d and 99e, we find two passing notes presented simultaneously, first as a part of the scale, then as a chromatic inflection involving notes not found in the scale. Next, as a logical expansion of this material, 99f shows a pair of double passing notes. Once again, the passage is in no way confusing harmonically because one always hears the notes moving from one point of rest to another. Finally, in 99g we have an extreme situation in which what appears to be a series of four triads (C major, D minor, B major, and C major) turns out to be a single C-major chord surrounding six passing tones. These are sometimes called passing chords. As always, the ear is the final arbiter, and does not hear the harmony on the second beat of the measure as a II chord because of the continued presence of the complete C-major chord in the bass. The notes on the third beat of the bar would seem to form a triad not found in the key of C, but once again they merely create a passing chord that in no way affects the stability of the underlying harmony. In each of the bars in example 99, the passing notes become more radical and more numerous, but the knowledgeable analyst would unhesitantly analyze the entire quotation as a single C-major chord.

For an interesting example of a theme constructed principally of passing chords, examine the opening of the last movement of Beethoven's Piano Sonata Op. 2 no. 3. When played *allegro assai* (very fast), one hears only the broad harmonic movement from the opening C-major chord to the F-major chord at the top of the run at the beginning of the third bar.

Passing notes can be found between successive statements of the same chord, and just as often between two separate chords. Thus, if one compares example 99a, which stayed within a C-major chord, with the passage in example 100, which moves from a C chord to a G chord, it is obvious that the function of the note F is not altered.

EXAMPLE 100

Another type of nonharmonic tone is the neighbor note, or auxiliary tone. It appears when a harmonic note moves a step or a half step away from its position, and then back again. If it moves up and back, the harmonic tone is called an upper neighbor; if it moves down and back, it is called a lower neighbor. The passage in example 101 represents a simplified version of the opening of Bach's Third Brandenburg Concerto. The theme is based fundamentally on a G-major chord sprinkled with an ample number of neighbor notes.

EXAMPLE 101

Like the passing note, the neighbor note may or may not be a member of the scale.

EXAMPLE 102

Also like the passing note, the neighbor note can appear between chord changes. Here, however, the second chord must be such as to allow the melody to move back to its original position.

EXAMPLE 103

More than one neighbor note can appear at the same time.

EXAMPLE 104

Appoggiaturas

When a passing note or a neighbor note is used, the harmonic tone appears on the beat with the chord, while the nonharmonic tone comes off the beat, or on a weak part of the bar. Quite often, however, a composer will create a particularly intense effect by sounding the nonharmonic note directly with the chord on an accented part of the bar. He will then resolve the note to the proper chord tone on the following beat or later in the bar. Although the *effect* of the chord has been altered considerably, harmonically nothing has been changed. With all their accidentals, the following bars still represent a sustained C-major chord. (Example 105.)

EXAMPLE 105

When the nonharmonic tone sounds on the beat with the chord, it is called an appoggiatura.[1] The only rule observed here is that if the appoggiatura sounds with the chord, the chord will normally not contain the note into which it will resolve. Thus, if one plays a D-major triad, but instead of the A uses a G♯ which will resolve to A, one should not sound the A in the chord at the same time. If the ear hears the G♯ simultaneously with the A, then it does not feel that the G♯ needs to resolve, since the A is there already completing the chord. If, on the other hand, the chord needs the A for completion, then the ear will appreciate the quality of suspense generated by the G♯, and anticipate its proper resolution to A. Thus, we see how the use of the appoggiatura increases the tension and forward movement of the harmony.

EXAMPLE 106

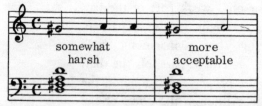

somewhat harsh

more acceptable

[1] Learn how to spell this word correctly *now!* Remember it contains two p's and two g's.

Suspensions and Anticipations

Sometimes a composer creates a momentary nonharmonic note by delaying the movement of a voice part from one chord to the next. In example 107, the top voice simply holds on to the tone from the first chord, while the other voices move on to the second. Thus, part of the first chord remains suspended into the second before it catches up by resolving to its proper place.

EXAMPLE 107

This type of nonharmonic tone is called a suspension.

In a similar way, one can reverse the idea of the suspension. Instead of one voice remaining behind while the other voices change, it can move ahead to a new chord tone while the others remain stationary. In example 108, the upper voice leaves one chord to anticipate the next in two different places.

EXAMPLE 108

This type of nonharmonic tone is appropriately called an anticipation.

In suspensions and anticipations, all the notes belong to either one chord or another. For a short moment, however, a note from one chord is sounded with the next. This is fundamentally different from the passing tone, neighbor tone or appoggiatura, since these do not belong to any chord, and may not even belong to the scale.

Echappée and Cambiata

Often when he uses suspensions, the composer will choose to decorate the melody by adding extra notes that further delay the resolution of the dissonant tone. Thus, one might find a variety of short melodic patterns appearing between the suspension and the note of resolution. These ornamental notes might move in any direction, and might consist of chord tones or not. They serve to increase the interest in the melodic line. A number of possible types are offered in example 109, and should be studied carefully.

EXAMPLE 109

Some of these ornaments have been classified by theorists, and given special names. One type, the *echappée,* is illustrated in example 109a and b. It occurs when the ornamented note first moves melodically in the opposite direction from that anticipated, i.e., it moves up when one expects it to move down, or vice versa. Another type, the *cambiata,* appears when the ornamented note moves too far in the expected direction before returning to the proper note of resolution. This is illustrated in example 109c and d. The distinction emphasized by these terms is rather technical, and perhaps fussy. One might define it more clearly by noting that *echappée* moves first by a step and then back by a skip, while the *cambiata* moves first by a skip and then back by a step. It is not vital that the specific term be identified as much as the overall type of melodic movement.

Harmonic Pedals

One very unusual type of nonharmonic tone is called the pedal, or pedal point. This occurs when a single note is sustained through a series of chords even though it only harmonizes with the first or the last. (Example 110.)

EXAMPLE 110

The rule governing the use of a pedal point demands that it begin and end its life as a part of the chord to which it belongs.

It cannot begin or end in a dissonant context, although during the chord changes it may very well produce a dissonant effect. It may take the form of a sustained note or a repeated note without affecting its harmonic character; it may appear in the upper, lower, or middle voice. It must, however, begin and end as a part of a consonant chord. (Example III.)

EXAMPLE III

Final Observations

Nonharmonic tones often appear within a smooth melodic context, and are approached by a stepwise motion. "Often," however, does not mean "always." On occasion, a composer may choose to create a special effect by jumping to a nonharmonic tone. The effect is somewhat startling because the ear cannot anticipate the dissonance. Thus, in example 112, an unusual melody is produced by the initial leap of an augmented 4th from F to B, with the B acting as a nonharmonic tone resolving to C.

EXAMPLE 112

F: I   IV$_4^6$ I   III   IV   I

The rule of procedure in these cases notes that if one jumps to a nonharmonic tone, then that note must resolve to its proper resolution. Example 113 is a variation of the first bars of the melody from example 112. It is unsatisfactory because the B is never resolved. As a result, the ear is unprepared for the E.

EXAMPLE 113

The variations in example 114, on the other hand, all reveal acceptable melodic movement because in each case the ear can account for the nonharmonic note by the direction in which it moves. No matter how devious the route, each dissonant note *eventually* resolves to its nearest chord tone.

EXAMPLE 114

Thus, in this short survey, we have isolated a considerable variety of nonharmonic tones. Their continued presence can alter the tonal effect of the chords, and the emotional content of a given passage. Their frequent appearance certainly complicates matters for the analyst. Yet insofar as they are not members of the fundamental chords, they do not alter the underlying harmonic framework for any given passage.

As a final example, here is a *pièce de résistance* of non-harmonic tones: the opening of the Prelude to Richard Strauss' opera *Ariadne auf Naxos*. The passage consists of a sustained C-major chord surrounded by a myriad of nonharmonic tones.[2] Can you identify them?

EXAMPLE 115

Sehr lebhaft und heiter

---

[2] Note the melodic movement from E♮ to F♯ in bars 3, 5, 7, etc., constituting an infraction of the rule prohibiting a leap from one unresolved nonharmonic tone to another.

etc.

EXERCISE

Define the following terms:

 Nonharmonic tone
 Passing note
 Neighbor note
 Suspension
 Anticipation
 Appoggiatura
 Cambiata
 Echappée
 Pedal point
 Passing chord
 Auxiliary tone

Check the following passages from J. S. Bach's *Well-Tempered Clavier,* Vol. II, and decide what types of nonharmonic tones are used. (Workbook, Section VIII, Exercise 7)

 Prelude 3, bars 1–3
 Prelude 6, bars 1–6
 Prelude 7, bars 1–4
 Prelude 9, bars 1–2, 5–6
 Prelude 13, bars 4–5
 Prelude 15, bars 1–6
 Prelude 17, bars 1–4
 Prelude 24, bars 1–4

11

THE MINOR SCALES

Major Versus Minor

THE FUNDAMENTAL BUILDING BLOCK for the major key is the major
triad. This triad, as we have noted, is simply a selection of the
overtones from any given bass note. The sounding of this triad
merely reinforces these overtones. The minor triad, on the other
hand, cannot be found as a part of the harmonic series.

EXAMPLE 116

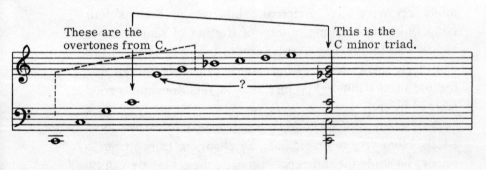

After examining the chart in example 116, one must conclude that the C-minor chord played on the piano in root
position will produce a slightly dissonant sound. This is
because the 3rd of the triad is an E♭, while the overtone from

the low C produces an E♮. This barely audible clash accounts for the special color of the chord, which might be described as darker or richer than the major triad. In certain contexts it will become dramatic or tragic in character.

Before examining the technical structure of the minor keys, let us first observe how they are most commonly used in Western music, particularly in contrast to the major keys. During the Baroque and Classical periods, the major tonality was certainly preferred. Only two of Mozart's 17 keyboard sonatas are written in minor, and only three of his 41 symphonies. Even these figures are deceptive, for a composition is traditionally said to be in minor only if the first movement is in that key. A symphony or a concerto beginning in minor will often use major keys for other movements, and may even end in major. Two of Beethoven's nine symphonies open in minor, which would seem to give us a figure of 22.2 per cent. In actuality, however, if one considers the 37 individual movements contained in these symphonies,[1] only seven are in minor, thus reducing the figure to a more accurate 18.9 per cent.

As the nineteenth century progressed, and the Romantic movement gained momentum, the expressive qualities of the minor key were more preferred. Thus, two of Brahms' four symphonies are in minor, a total of five out of sixteen movements. This brings the percentage up to 31.2. As a result of this admittedly small survey, we have some evidence to indicate that the use of the minor key increased as the Romantic period reached its end.

Very often, composers go out of their way to create special effects, often very dramatic ones, by changing from major to minor. To study the differences between these keys we can do no better than to listen to the examples listed below so that the effect of the alterations can be noted.

---

[1] All of Beethoven's symphonies have four movements each except the Sixth, the *Pastoral,* which has five.

1. The overture to Mozart's opera *Don Giovanni* (Don Juan) begins with a slow introduction in minor. The dramatic effect is heightened by the use of chromatic chords. When the introduction ends, the music changes to major, and the tempo increases to *Allegro*. The rest of the overture remains fast, light, and diatonic.

2. To note the effect of the opposite change, this time from major to minor, one should listen to the Prelude to Bizet's opera *Carmen*. Here the first part is fast, and in a major key. At the very end, however, a striking passage occurs in a slow tempo in a minor key. The sudden change is particularly effective and quite dramatic.

3. In both cases above, the major tonality appeared in a fast tempo, and the minor in a slow one. One should compare the first movement of Beethoven's "Moonlight" Sonata, Op. 17 no. 2, with the final movement to note the difference between a slow movement in minor and a fast one in the same key. This comparison is particularly meaningful here because both movements use the same thematic material in the form of an arpeggio on the tonic chord. Yet the change of tempo produces a considerable contrast between the two themes. (See example 117.)

After comparing these movements, one should then listen to the entire Sonata, since between the outer movements there appears a middle movement in a major key. This interlude contrasts so effectively with the others that Franz Liszt referred to it poetically as "a flower between two abysses."

4. Finally, one should note the same melody as it appears in both major and minor forms. One of the best examples can be found in Tchaikovsky's Fifth Symphony (example 118). This work opens with a theme in minor that will recur in the following movements. At the beginning of the last movement, it is transformed into major. The effect of this transformation is most brilliant, and very strong.

EXAMPLE 117

a. First movement, opening

Adagio sostenuto

sempre **pp** *e senza sordino*

b. Third movement, opening

Presto agitato

EXAMPLE 118

a. First movement, opening

Andante

b. Fourth movement, opening

Andante maestoso

The Three Minor Scales

Fundamentally, each minor key uses as its basis a scale and
key signature derived from a major key. These two keys, one
major and one minor, become associated together because they
share the same scale and the same key signature. As a result,
they will also share a number of the same chords. The minor
key standing in this relationship to C major is A minor. A
minor is then known as the "relative minor" scale of C major.

We can begin our study of the minor keys with the so-called "natural" minor scale, that is, the one borrowed untouched from the relative major key. Example 119 is the natural minor scale of A, with a characteristic melody derived from it.

EXAMPLE 119

a. Natural minor scale

b. Melody

This type of scale is often found in folk tunes, as the theme above may suggest. In the natural minor scale, half steps appear between 2–3, and between 5–6. This contrasts with the major scale, where the half steps appear between 3–4 and 7–8. The problem with the natural minor scale is rooted in the absence of the half step between 7–8. If a G♯ could be substituted for the G♮, then the melody could be harmonized in a more traditional manner. Compare the final phrase in example 119b with the two versions in example 120.

EXAMPLE 120

The first harmonization, a I-III-I progression, accentuates the modal character of the melody. The second version introduces the G♯, allowing for the use of an E-major chord and a more traditional I-V-I progression that emphasizes tonal values.

Yet, the modal harmonization is very attractive, and perhaps even more appealing than the more conventional tonal chords. This may be true, but in one sense it is beside the point. Remember, we are not passing judgment here; we are not suggesting that one scale pattern could be more beautiful than another. We are merely examining a tradition of composition as it was practiced during the eighteenth and nineteenth centuries. At that time, it was mandatory to establish the key and affirm the keynote by keeping the half step between the seventh and eighth degrees of the scale. And so, into the placid natural minor scale of A we must introduce a G♯. This will allow us to use the major form of the dominant chord (E-G♯-B) in a strong tonal cadence. We have thus produced a second type of minor scale, known appropriately as the "harmonic" minor. (Example 121.)

EXAMPLE 121

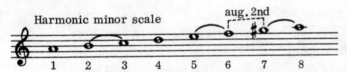

The raised seventh degree, however, seems to produce more problems than it solves. Although it may have certain advantages harmonically, it becomes very exotic melodically. Half steps appear between 2-3, 5-6, and 7-8, resulting in an augmented 2nd (F♮-G♯) between 6-7. Once again, this is in itself not unattractive, but it seems more suited to Eastern melodies than to those of the Western tradition. As a result, this new difficulty must be removed through a further alteration of the scale.

The seventh degree must be raised if it is to act as a leading tone, and move to 8. It need not be raised if it moves down to 6, however, because then it does not act as a leading tone. Thus, if a melody descends, it may very well use the notes A-G-F-E. If it ascends, however, and needs the G♯ to move from 7–8, one should avoid the augmented 2nd between 6–7 by raising the sixth degree as well. Thus, in our final alteration, we have arrived at the "melodic" minor scale that ascends in one pattern and descends in another. (Example 122.)

EXAMPLE 122

Melodic minor scale

1 2 3 4 5 6 7 8 7 6 5 4 3 2 1

This final version looks rather formidable, but is actually ideal. It manages to combine the best virtues of both the natural and harmonic minor scales without including any of their "vices." The melodic minor scale now contains half steps between 2–3 and 7–8 ascending, and between 6–5 and 3–2 descending. All the other intervals are whole steps.

The relationship between A minor and C major will stand as the model for all major and minor scales. In each case the minor keynote can be found on the sixth degree of the major scale, or on the tone a minor 3rd below the major tonic. Thus, one can construct two circles of fifths, one inside the other, to represent the complete set of major and minor scales and their tonal relationships to each other. (See p. 157.)

EXERCISE

Be able to construct natural, harmonic, and melodic minor scales beginning on any note. Then, when this has been accomplished, prepare a chart of all the minor scales in their

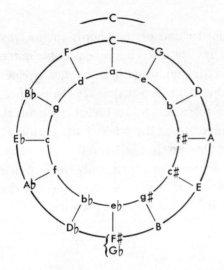

melodic form, written the same way as the major scales previously, beginning with the scale pattern, and following it with the key signature borrowed from the relative major tonality. Example 123 shows the G-minor scale as it should be written.

EXAMPLE 123

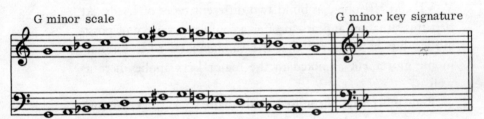

Start with A minor, and then go around the circle of fifths. (Workbook, Section IX, Exercise 10)

Harmony in the Minor Scale

Now that the complex problem of the construction of the minor scales has been completed, we can turn our attention to a bigger problem: the construction of the chords themselves. Since the minor scale contains not seven but nine possible notes, including two different sixth and seventh degrees, a greater variety of chords is available than in a major key. In practice, however, not every chord turns out to be useful. In general, chords that can be constructed from the notes of the harmonic minor scale are preferred. One rarely finds chords in a minor key using the raised sixth degree; one occasionally finds chords using the lowered seventh degree. Example 124 shows all the triads that can be constructed in the C-minor tonality.

EXAMPLE 124

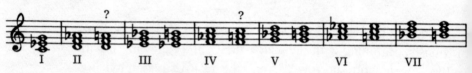

At a glance, one can see a great many types of chords. Of the thirteen noted above, five are major, four are minor, three are diminished, and one is augmented. On scale degrees II, III, IV, V, VI, and VII one can build two different types of triads. At first this situation appears to offer a confusing variety of possibilities, but be reassured that the fundamental rules for harmonic movement as noted in the major keys applies here as well.

Remember that the raised sixth degree (A♮ in C minor) rarely appears in the minor key. Thus, the II chord above will almost invariably be found in its diminished form D-F-A♭, and the IV chord in its minor form F-A♭-C. The A♮ remains a melodic tone rather than a harmonic one, and is used when a voice part moves to B♮. This reduces the number of practical chords in the minor scale from thirteen to eleven. Now let us see how these are most frequently used by composers.

The minor scale receives its fundamental coloring from the lowered 3rd of the tonic chord. There is certainly no restriction as to the use of this triad. The II chord, on the other hand, presents us with some items to consider more carefully. In its most common form, D-F-Ab, it is a diminished triad. We have come across only one other diminished triad so far, that appearing on the seventh degree of the major scale. There, one tended to place the chord in first inversion, and to double the third degree, thus reducing the emphasis on the outer tritone. This was particularly necessary since the lower note of the tritone was the leading tone of the scale. The same diminished chord appearing on II in minor, however, needs no special treatment, since the diminished 5th, D-Ab, is not in a critical position in the scale. Neither of these notes is a leading tone, and therefore neither exerts a special will of its own. Thus, this triad will often appear in root position, and with the root doubled. (Example 125.)

EXAMPLE 125

I　　II　　I⁶　V　　I

As has been noted previously, the II chord virtually never appears in minor in the form D-F-A♮.

The III chord, on the other hand, can be found in two forms: the first major (Eb-G-Bb) and the second augmented (Eb-G-B♮). When should one be used, and when the other? At first thought, one might assume that the major form of the chord would be more common than the augmented form, but this is not necessarily the case. The deciding factor here is the difference in the function of the Bb and the B♮ within the C-minor scale. B♮ is the leading tone; Bb is not. Thus, if the chord contains a B♮, it tends to move to one containing a C as the proper resolution for this tone. The augmented form of the III chord in minor thus tends to act like a dominant, and to move to the tonic. This aspect of the chord is often enhanced by its use in the first inversion, with the dominant of the scale in the bass. (Example 126.)

EXAMPLE 126

On the other hand, the major form of the III chord does not use the leading tone, and thus acts in a freer manner, appearing in the root position, and moving not only to I, but just as often to IV, VI, or some other scale degree. This chord is, after all, the relative major triad [2] and as such will appear more often in a minor key than the corresponding mediant triad in a major key as shown in example 127.

EXAMPLE 127

[2] It is the tonic chord of the relative major key E♭.

The IV chord invariably appears in its minor form, and is used freely and frequently. Its color is especially rich, and it appears more often in root position than in inversion.

EXAMPLE 128

The V chord again presents us with an unusual situation. Here a significant distinction must be made between the true dominant chord (G-B♮-D), which includes the all-important leading tone, and the so-called minor V chord (G-B♭-D), which will not act like a dominant at all. A dominant chord *must* contain a leading tone, and therefore even in C minor, with B♭ in the key signature, the B♮ must appear in the score when the dominant is used. This triad must remain major, and as such it will act in exactly the same manner as the dominant chord in the major key, It will most often resolve directly to the tonic. (Example 129.)

EXAMPLE 129

The minor V chord will not act like a dominant at all, and will most often move down a 3rd to an E♭ chord, or up a 2nd to A♭. It should *not* move to the tonic. One often reads an admonition never to use the minor chord on V, since the B♭ cancels the B♮ leading tone, and thus weakens the central position of the tonic. This may sound valid in the abstract, except that composers have never gone out of their way to avoid using the minor V chord. (Although the key signature for the entire movement in example 130 indicates F major, this particular passage is in C minor.)

EXAMPLE 130

The VI chord is most often built on the lowered scale degree, and thus appears as a major triad. Composers often use it in the first inversion with the tonic in the bass, and from this position it will probably move to the tonic chord. In root position it will act like any strong chord and tend to move down a 3rd to IV, since it obviously cannot move up a perfect 4th to D♭ and remain within the diatonic scale.

EXAMPLE 131

$$\text{I} \qquad \text{VI}^6 \qquad \text{I} \qquad \text{VI} \qquad \text{IV} \qquad \text{V} \qquad \text{I}$$

The VI chord is not often built on the raised degree A♮. When it is, it will be treated in a manner similar to the diminished chord on II, and used in root position. It could resolve either to ♭VII (B♭ major), or to II or V. (Example 132.)

EXAMPLE 132

$$\text{I} \qquad ♮\text{VI} \quad ♭\text{VII} \quad \text{V} \qquad \text{I}$$

This leaves us at last with only the two VI chords to consider: the major triad built on B♭, and the diminished triad built on B♮. The diminished triad has already been noted in the major scale, and is used here in the same manner. The triad on the lowered seventh degree, however, exhibits the same characteristics as the minor V chord in that it does not contain the leading tone. Thus, when it appears, it most often moves up a

4th to the major triad on III. In this form, it acts as a dominant of the relative major key. (Example 133.)

EXAMPLE 133

I   V   I   bVII   III   IV   V   I

All these rules may at first exposure seem overwhelming and confusing, but on closer familiarity it will be seen they are based on a few fundamental principles. Some of these can be isolated and considered separately. The difference between the major and minor tonalities lies in the III, VI, and VII scale degrees, all of which are a half step lower in minor. The composer writing in the minor key tends to stress the differences between the modes, and to accentuate these notes. The lowered III offers no problem, since the raised III will not normally appear at all. VI and VII, however, may appear in either form. Although the lowered VI tends to be preferred in most cases, the raised VII appears most often because of its leading tone qualities. The raised VI is avoided because it tends to remove the "minor" qualities from the music. Lowered VII, on the other hand, is not avoided, but appears less frequently because it has no leading-tone qualities. It tends to support the relative major key, since it acts as its dominant. Thus, B♮ is the leading tone of C minor, while B♭ is the dominant of E♭ major.

Music written in the minor keys should be studied to see how the most common progressions are used. No amount of intellectual speculation can ever replace familiarity with the actual scores themselves. After all, theory is only presented as it is deduced from the works of the masters. Masterworks, on the other hand, are not constructed by following the advice offered in theory books.

Interchange of Major and Minor Harmonies

One final point should be considered before we leave the subject of the minor keys. This is the interrelation between the major and minor modes. Composers frequently borrow chords from one mode to use them in another. Most often, it is the composition written in the major key which will introduce a chord from the parallel minor.[3] The reverse situation, in which a composition in a minor key borrows harmonies from the major, occurs less frequently. Some of these borrowings are so common that they can be considered now, even though technically they come under the heading of chromatic harmony, and as such lie outside the considerations of diatonic harmony.

Probably the most typical method of borrowing appears when the composer introduces a minor subdominant chord into a cadence in a major key. The effect is so commonplace as to sound somewhat sentimental. (Example 134.)

EXAMPLE 134

I   V   I   IV   I

[3] The parallel minor is that key built from the same note as the major scale. Thus, C major is the parallel major key to C minor; E♭ major is the relative major key.

EXAMPLE 135

Allegretto moderato

etc.

Another common device appears when the composer remains on a single chord, most often the tonic, moving back and forth between its major and minor forms. The change in tone color produced by the shift of one note a half step is quite effective. Example 135 contains one of the most well-known examples of this device.

EXAMPLE 136

One final example of borrowing from one mode to another can be found in many compositions of Johann Sebastian Bach. After writing a composition in minor, Bach will often end the work on a *major* tonic chord. He apparently felt that this form of the triad afforded a more stable ending for a piece, as indeed it does. The effect is found so frequently as to practically substitute for the composer's signature. (Example 136.)

EXERCISE

Check through the first volume of Bach's *Well-Tempered Clavier* and note how many of the Preludes written in minor keys (the even-numbered Preludes) end on a major chord. (Workbook, Section IX, Exercise 18)

Define the following:
    Natural minor scale
    Relative minor scale
    Harmonic minor scale
    Melodic minor scale
    Parallel minor scale
    Minor V chord

12

SEVENTH AND
NINTH CHORDS

THE POSSIBILITY of increasing the "length" of chords by adding notes beyond the root, 3rd, and 5th, opens up an area for exploration that has not yet been considered. Since chords are theoretically built in 3rds, they can be extended by taking any triad and adding one or more 3rds above it. A 3rd above the 5th of the chord is the 7th, and another 3rd above this is the 9th. This terminology defines the interval between the note and the root. The chords produced this way are appropriately called 7th and 9th chords.

EXAMPLE 137

| Tone | Interval | Triad | 7th chord | 9th chord |
| | (3rd) | (root, 3rd,5th) | | |

The resulting sound increases the complexity of the harmony. The 7th and 9th chords are classified as dissonances because of the unstable intervals appearing between the root and the upper notes. These dissonances, however, cannot be classified as non-harmonic tones since they form a part of the chord. As dissonances, however, they must be treated with respect, and handled carefully.

Types of 7th Chords

Let us begin by considering 7th chords purely as constructions, before their functions within the scales are noted. In our survey of intervals, we identified both a major and a minor 3rd. We also noted four types of triads: major, minor, diminished, and augmented. Thus, from a purely theoretical point of view, one should be able to combine any triad with any 3rd in order to produce eight different types of 7th chords. (Example 138.)

EXAMPLE 138

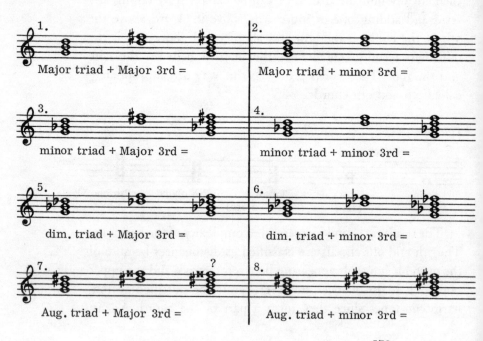

Once again we note that everything that is theoretically possible is not really practical. Augmented triads, for example, are so unstable, and appear so infrequently in diatonic music, that a 7th chord built from an augmented triad is a genuine rarity. This leaves six chords, which can be classified as follows with their most common designations.

1. A major triad with a major 3rd added. This is called a major 7th chord, and can be found on I and IV in major, and on III and VI in minor.

2. A major triad with a minor 3rd added. This is called a dominant 7th chord, and can be found on V in both major and minor. A similar type of chord, but one that is not a true dominant, also appears on ♭VII in minor.

3. A minor triad with a major 3rd added. This has no specific name, and can theoretically be found on I in minor. We will discover later, however, that this is perhaps not a 7th chord at all.

4. A minor triad with a minor 3rd added. This is called a minor 7th (or sometimes a small 7th) chord, and can be found on II, III, and VI in major, and on IV in minor.

5. A diminished triad with a major 3rd added. This is sometimes called a half-diminished 7th chord, and can be found on VII in major, and on II in minor.

6. A diminished triad with a minor 3rd added. This is called a diminished 7th chord, and can be found on VII in minor.

EXERCISE

Be able to construct any of these chords on any given pitch. (Workbook, Section X, Exercise 1) Be able to recognize their characteristic sounds as they are played. Finally, given a root note, be able to sing the notes of any of these chords.

Treatment of 7th Chords

Example 139 is a list of all the available 7th chords within the major and the minor keys. Those which appear infrequently have been indicated in parentheses. Remember, not every chord that is theoretically possible turns out to be practical.

EXAMPLE 139

a. 7th chords in Major

$I^7 \quad II^7 \quad III^7 \quad IV^7 \quad V^7 \quad VI^7 \quad VII^7$

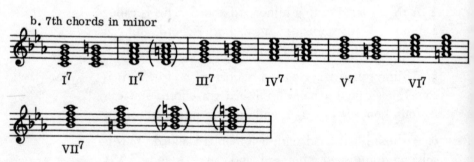

b. 7th chords in minor

$I^7 \quad II^7 \quad III^7 \quad IV^7 \quad V^7 \quad VI^7$

VII^7

Let us now discuss some general problems, and from this proceed through the list to note specific problems concerning individual chords. Since the interval created between the root and 7th is dissonant, this dissonance is normally resolved by moving the 7th down the scale one step into the next chord. (Example 140.)

EXAMPLE 140

7th Resolution   F7 ——→ Bb⁶₄

In some of these chords, notably those found on V and VII, there results an additional dissonance, the diminished 5th, between two of the notes. This dissonance is strong enough to demand that both notes move toward a proper resolution. The notes of the diminished 5th resolve inward to form a 3rd, while those of the augmented 4th resolve outward to form a 6th. (Example 141.)

EXAMPLE 141

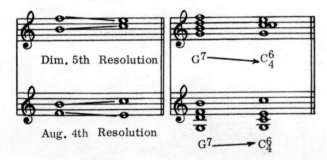

Dim. 5th Resolution   G⁷ ——→ C⁶₄

Aug. 4th Resolution   G⁷ ——→ C⁶₄

The interval of the 9th is treated similarly, and resolved through the movement of the upper note down a scale degree, just as in the 7th chord. (Example 142.)

EXAMPLE 142

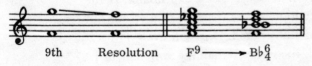

9th   Resolution   F⁹ ——→ Bb⁶₄

Thus, one commonly finds at least one tone of a 7th chord dissonant in relationship to another, and requiring special resolution. In the case of the VII₇ chord, or the dominant 9th, three of the notes are dissonant (B, F, and A or A♭ in C). These must all be treated carefully, and resolved properly. (Example 143.)

EXAMPLE 143

Aug. 5th Resolution   7th Resolution   B7———►C

The next general problem concerns four-part writing, and the doubling of chord tones. At first thought, these might not seem to offer any problems at all, since only when four voices sound a three-note chord would there be any need to double tones at all. If four voices sound a four-note chord, one might assume that each voice could take one note. In a 9th chord, consisting as it does of five notes, the problem would be to decide what note to eliminate.

EXAMPLE 144

Consecutive octaves poor   Better!

G⁷ ———► C

As with the triad, the note most easily expendable is the 5th. One often finds a situation where the root of a 7th or 9th chord is doubled, and the 5th omitted. One will even on occasion find the 3rd omitted, the chord remaining coherent in its context. Obviously the 7th cannot be doubled, since it is a tendency tone. If two voices sounding the same note must resolve it in a specific direction, consecutive octaves would result. (Example 144.)

All these precautions probably sound excessive, since we have not even begun to examine the individual chords as they appear on the various scale degrees. These rules of procedure, however, are consistently employed. It is astonishing to find how quickly they become second nature.

The next general problem concerns inversions. In a four-note chord, there are now three possible inversions, with the 3rd, 5th, or 7th appearing in the bass. Example 145 shows these inversions with their proper figured bass notations placed beneath them.

EXAMPLE 145

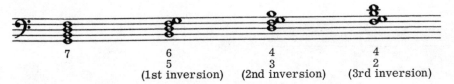

7   6   4   4
               5   3   2
           (1st inversion)   (2nd inversion)   (3rd inversion)

The first inversion poses no problem, and can be used freely. The precautions originally noted for the second inversion of triads still hold true here. Second inversions, either $\frac{6}{4}$ or $\frac{4}{3}$ chords, are generally avoided except at cadential points. When they appear in the middle of a phrase, they are found on a weak beat, and with the bass moving smoothly both to and from this chord. (Example 146.)

EXAMPLE 146

C: I   III^7 I   I$^6_4$ II$^4_3$ V   I

The third inversion of the 7th chord, on the other hand, is not uncommon in practice. It creates a very strong sound, since an unstable note appears in the bass. The ear, however, has little difficulty comprehending the position of this note, and hearing the 7th in the bass. It is very important to resolve the 7th down a step to its proper note of resolution. In the bass, the note of resolution is invariably the 3rd of the next chord. To rephrase this in technical language, one notes that the bass of a $\frac{4}{2}$ chord should resolve down a scale degree to form a 6 or $\frac{6}{5}$ chord. (Example 147.)

EXAMPLE 147

C: I$^6_4$ V$^4_2$ I6

If a 7th chord offers the possibility of a third inversion, then it would seem to follow that a 9th chord could appear in a fourth inversion, i.e., with the 9th in the bass. This, however, is not the case. Somehow, the ear can accept the 9th of a chord most easily when it appears in an upper voice. Even in a middle voice, it becomes difficult to comprehend, but when placed in the bass it usually sounds "wrong." The effect is very curious. (Example 148.)

EXAMPLE 148

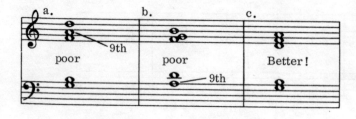

a.   b.   c.

poor   poor   Better!

The first time a 9th chord appeared in Western music in the fourth inversion was in Schoenberg's *Verklärte Nacht* (Transfigured Night), written in 1899 at the very end of the tonal period. It does not sound questionable in context since the chords surrounding it are all unstable. Yet Schoenberg received considerable criticism even at this time for his harmonic boldness. (Example 149.)

EXAMPLE 149

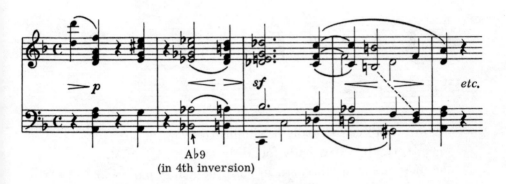

Ab9
(in 4th inversion)

Seventh Chords in the Major Keys

With these general observations out of the way, let us review the various 7th chords as they appear in the major scales. This discussion will not include 9th chords, since these are not commonly found on all scale degrees, and since observations noted about 7th chords will apply to them as well.

The I_7 chord rarely appears in an unaltered form, i.e., as a normal part of the diatonic scale. The tonic is fundamentally a stable tone, and does not ideally support the unstable qualities of a 7th chord. Also, the tendency of the leading tone to resolve *up* fights the tendency of the 7th to resolve *down*. Often, what appears to be a I_7 chord turns out to be a suspension from the previous dominant. (Example 150.)

EXAMPLE 150

Not a I⁷ chord

Thus, this chord can virtually be eliminated from the list.

The II₇ chord is frequently found. In fact, outside of V₇ it is the most common 7th chord in both the major and minor scales. It usually appears in the first inversion, moving directly to I_4^6 or V₇ as a part of a strong cadential figure. This progression is very common in the works of Mozart (Example 151.)

EXAMPLE 151

D: I_4^6 V⁷ I_4^6

There are no special problems attached to the use of III$_7$ or IV$_7$ in major. These chords can be found in the works of nineteenth-century composers who preferred a more chromatic idiom, but are otherwise not frequently encountered. (Example 152.)

EXAMPLE 152

The V$_7$ chord is the most significant 7th chord. It is often expanded into elaborate passages in conjunction with the I chord, and is used as the penultimate chord for most compositions. (Example 153a and b.)

The dominant 9th is very expressive in the major key, producing a rich, full sound. (Example 154.)

Even in major, the dominant 9th often borrows the lowered sixth scale degree from the minor, although the reverse procedure almost never occurs. The effect of the lowered 9th is very expressive, and at times dramatic. (Example 155.)

EXAMPLE 153

a. End of first movement.

b. End of second movement.

Ab: I   V$^6_5$ 7   I   V$^6_5$ 7

I   V$^6_5$ I

decrescendo   *pp*

EXAMPLE 154

Andante molto cantabile ed espressivo

mezza voce

E:

The VI₇ chord does not appear too frequently. When it does, it is found most often in the first inversion, with the tonic appearing in the bass. In popular music, one often finds a tonic

EXAMPLE 155

chord with an added 6th. On paper, this looks just like
a VI$^6_5$ chord, but in sound functions as a tonic. It is not found
in traditional eighteenth and nineteenth-century music. (Example 156.)

The VII$_7$ chord is particularly useful. Just as the VII triad
functions as a dominant, VII$_7$ acts in a similar manner. If one

compares the V_7 chord G-B-D-F in the key of C with the VII
triad B-D-F one can see why the latter acts as a dominant.
It is in fact a dominant 7th without the root. How is it possible
to analyze the appearance of a chord without a root? Although
this type of thinking is not too common in theoretical writings,
it is by no means unknown. The effect of. the .V_7 chord is
determined not only by the root, G, but by the 5th and 7th,
B and F. After all, suppose you heard only a sustained C-major
triad. You could hardly be sure of its function, whereas if you
heard a diminished triad B-D-F, you would be much more
certain of the key center. Therefore, one can in this case consider the V_7, or the VII triad, or the VII_7, as fundamental for
the establishment of the key.

EXAMPLE 156

In order to clarify this point, study the seven different chords
in example 157, all of which function in one way or another as
dominants to C.

EXAMPLE 157

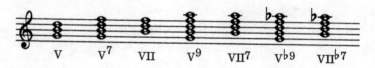

184

Thus, just as a I_7 chord does not exist on a practical level even though theoretically it can be constructed, so the diminished triad on VII does not act as an independent chord. It is in reality an incomplete dominant 7th. Similarly, the VII_7 chord, with a natural or lowered 7th (in major or in minor), can be considered an incomplete dominant 9th. Remember, one determines the nature of a chord not by its appearance on the printed page, but by its function within a musical context.

Seventh Chords in the Minor Keys

Let us now examine the various 7th chords as they appear in the minor scales. The I_7 with the lowered 7th tends to act like any other 7th chord, while the raised 7th appears only as a suspension from a V-I progression. Thus, like the I_7 in major, it exists more as a theoretical possibility than an actual one.

EXAMPLE 158

Am: I_4^6 V   I (not a I^7)

The II_7 chord invariably occurs with the lowered sixth of the scale degree. Like the unadorned II chord in minor, it may appear in root position as well as in first inversion. It is very strong and colorful, and is used very frequently. It contains the interval of the diminished 5th between the root and 5th. Since neither of these notes is a leading tone of the scale, the resolution is slightly different than that of the VII chord in major. Usually the upper note, the 5th of the triad, moves down a half step, but the lower note, the root of the chord, instead of moving up a half step, moves up a 4th, as in the example 159.

EXAMPLE 159

Cm: I   II⁷   V   I

Just as the II chord with the raised 5th (D-F-A♮) is rarely found in minor, so the III₇ with the raised 5th (E♭-G-B♮-D) is almost never found. It would produce a rather dissonant chord, since it would consist of an augmented triad plus a major 7th. The III₇ is most often used in minor with the lowered 5th. (Example 160.)

EXAMPLE 160

Cm: I   IV   VII   III⁷   IV   V   7   I

The IV₇ chord presents a more interesting problem. It appears in C minor both with A♭ and A♮ but with the following differences in function. The first form, with the lowered 3rd

Ab, is the IV₇ proper, and functions as any well-behaved sub-dominant. The second form, with the A♮, takes on the contour of a dominant 7th chord built on F. It acts as a V₇ of Bb, and almost invariably moves in this direction. (Example 161.)

EXAMPLE 161

The dominant 7th chord in minor maintains the major 3rd, since this is the leading tone. Thus, in C major as well as C minor, the dominant 7th chord must be spelled G-B♮-D-F. A common mistake in writing in the minor key for the first time is to forget to raise the seventh degree of the scale when using a dominant or dominant 7th chord, since this is not indicated automatically by the key signature.

One sometimes, but not often, finds a minor V₇ chord (G-Bb-D-F in C minor). This, however, poses some peculiar problems, and need not be considered at present.

The VI₇ chord in minor takes the form of a major 7th chord, for which no specific precautions need be considered. When, however, the VI₇ chord is built on the raised sixth degree (A♮-C-Eb-G in C minor), then it tends to move to Bb just as if it were a VII₇ chord in that key. In all cases where a chord takes on any form of dominant harmony in any key, it tends to move toward its own tonic. (Example 162.)

EXAMPLE 162

Cm: I   VI$^6_5$ ♮VI♮$^6_5$ VII   I   V   I

This principle appears again with the 7th chord built on the lowered seventh degree in minor, i.e., Bb-D-F-Ab. A bVII$_7$ of C, functions as the V$_7$ of Eb, and, as a result, even within C minor, tends to move to Eb. In fact, as we shall see in Chapter 13, such a chord is normally not even called a bVII$_7$ chord, but rather a V$_7$ of Eb, or a V$_7$ of III. While this type of analysis may seem rather complicated at first, it certainly defines the functional characteristics of the chord most accurately. (Example 163.)

EXAMPLE 163

Cm: I   IV   VII^7 III   VI   II^6 V^7 I
              (Eb:V^7 I)

A more normal VII$_7$ chord in minor is built on the raised scale degree (B♮-D-F-Ab in C minor). It acts as a true VII chord, i.e., as a form of the dominant, and usually moves to the tonic. It is most commonly found in the first inversion. (Example 164.)

EXAMPLE 164

Cm: I   III   IV   VII$^{\natural 6}_{5}$ I$^6_4$ V   I

Conclusion

At this point, assuming all the material of the preceding chapters has been mastered, the entire area of diatonic harmony has been covered. Carefully review the work to be sure of all the material in each of the areas. Be able to identify all these harmonies as they appear in compositions heard and in exercises played in class. Be able to write progressions involving chords in all positions both in a keyboard style and in four-part harmony without breaking any of the rules laid down for proper voice-leading. Be able to recognize these harmonies as they appear in score.

To sum up, the music in each of the areas below must be able to be heard, written, and analyzed.

1. All the intervals from the minor 2nd to the major 10th, both harmonic and melodic, ascending and descending.

2. All the key signatures and all forms of scale patterns for the major and minor keys.

3. All the triads and 7th chords in all positions and inversions as they appear in all the major and minor keys.

4. Standard progressions of two or more chords in all keys.

Ideally, one should be able to hear a short passage played on the piano, and, upon being told the key, be able to write out the passage. Now, in truth, this ideal is not easily achieved. One spends a lifetime learning how to hear music more and more carefully and perceptively. One never gets to the point when one can say, "Now my ear is trained; now I hear everything that occurs within a piece of music." Of course, some of us are born with very sensitive ears, with so-called "perfect pitch," and can identify chords with relative ease, while some of us only learn this over a period of time given to much study and concentration. Be assured that the ear is one of the most easily trained of the human organs. Almost every music student has the experience of being at first unable to distinguish between one type of harmony and another, and then after a time finding himself able to distinguish them without any effort. One of the great joys of listening to music and loving it through a lifetime comes from its inexhaustible nature. Our pleasure can continually increase as we grow in knowledge and understanding.

EXERCISE

Define:
    Seventh chord
    Ninth chord
    Major seventh chord
    Dominant seventh chord
    Minor seventh chord
    Small seventh chord
    Half-diminished seventh chord
    Diminished seventh chord

PART IV

Introduction to
Chromatic Harmony

13

SECONDARY DOMINANT
CHORDS

WITH THE PRINCIPAL MATERIAL of diatonic harmony summarized
in the preceding chapters, this short conclusion can suggest
a number of further possibilities, and bring us to the next major
area of study, that of *chromatic harmony*. These two areas are
not at all separate from each other, since many aspects of
chromatic harmony have already been covered in preceding
chapters. One cannot discuss minor keys, with their raised and
lowered scale degrees, without examining some aspect of
chromatic harmony; one cannot discuss the possibility of
borrowing a note from a minor scale and using it in the major
key without examining another aspect of chromatic harmony;
one cannot even discuss the relationships between keys without
touching on this same area.

In theory, diatonic harmony limits itself to the seven notes
of the scale. Since the octave can be divided into twelve semi-
tones, however, there remain five notes that do not belong
to any individual scale. Up to this point in our studies, all the
chords in the major keys, and many of those in the minor
keys, remained within the diatonic area controlled by the
seven scale degrees. One might then define the study of

chromatic harmony as the study of the use of all twelve notes of the chromatic scale within any given key. Those composers whose styles tend to be predominantly diatonic are Handel, Mozart, and Haydn, all from the eighteenth century. Those who seem most preoccupied with chromatic harmony are Bach in the early eighteenth century, and Wagner, Brahms, Richard Strauss, and Mahler in the late nineteenth century. The historical period most closely associated with diatonic music was the Classical period, the latter half of the eighteenth century, while that most closely associated with chromatic harmony is the late Romantic and post-Romantic period, at the end of the nineteenth century.

Without a doubt, the most common form of chromatic harmony is the secondary dominant chord. The principle behind this construction is simple enough: any major or minor triad appearing on a diatonic scale degree can for a moment take on the qualities of a tonic, and follow its own dominant or dominant 7th chord. To explain this in another way, one might say that within the key of C a chord may appear which is not a part of that key, but which is rather a dominant of D, E, F, G, or of any other triad within that scale. This chord is then called a V of II, a V of III, etc. The function is sometimes abbreviated as V/II or V/III. (Example 165.)

EXAMPLE 165

The use of these chords considerably expands harmonic possibilities, and adds to the overall richness of the musical vocabulary employed. It enables one to harmonize the notes of the chromatic scale with considerable ease, and without ever moving out of the original key. (Example 166.)

EXAMPLE 166

C: I V⁷/II II V⁷/III III V⁷/IV IV V⁷/V V V⁷/VI VI V⁷/IV IV V⁷ I

Only in one place can a secondary dominant not be used in major, and that is before the VII chord. Since this is not a stable triad, it is not normally reinforced by its own dominant. Aside from this, the other six scale degrees in the major key can without restriction be preceded by their own dominants.

A slight problem is raised through the introduction of the chromatic note itself. A V/II in C is an A₇ chord, A-C♯-E-G. The introduction of a C♯ could easily produce a problem in voice-leading. If the chord before the V/II contains a C♮, then most ideally the voice sounding this note should move to the C♯. Thus, when the C♯ resolves properly to D, the part will have moved chromatically C♮-C♯-D. (Example 167.)

EXAMPLE 167
Smooth voice leading.

C: I   V⁷/II   II

195

If, however, the C♮ is in one voice part and the C♯ in another, then a so-called "cross relationship" or "false relation" appears, creating a dissonant interval from the one to the other. (Example 168.)

EXAMPLE 168

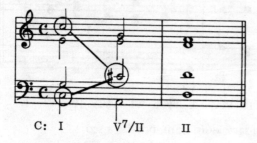

C: I   V⁷/II   II

Although theorists discourage the use of such a cross relationship, examples can be found in the works of many composers. (Example 169.)

EXAMPLE 169

Cross relationship

The only rule to be generally considered is that one should not normally make an awkward leap to a chromatic note, as it renders it rather difficult to sing and to hear. Composers, however, have always been more concerned with the resolution of dissonances than with their preparation. What follows is thus more important than what proceeds.

Although secondary dominants can be used freely in major, their use in minor becomes a bit more complicated because of the altered scale degrees. In general the rule seems to hold that a triad can be preceded by its own dominant if it is normally major or minor, and if the dominant tone appears as a scale degree within the key. Thus, a number of secondary dominants in the minor scale do not work out too well on a practical level.

The V/II chord is not very successful here, since II is normally a diminished triad, and since its dominant is a melodic rather than a harmonic tone. The progression in example 170 does not occur very frequently.

EXAMPLE 170

If III appears as a major triad in a minor key, it may be preceded by its dominant. This is very common, as III is the relative major. One seems to be able to move from chords in a minor key to those in the relative major without effort. (Example 171.)

The V/IV chord occurs quite frequently, particularly at the end of a composition. Since most pieces move to the dominant near the beginning or the middle, it would seem natural to move in the opposite direction (to the subdominant) near the end. (Example 172.)

EXAMPLE 171

Em: I V7 I V7/III III V7 I

EXAMPLE 172

G: I   V7/IV   IV$^6_4$

sf   p   cresc.

V   I   V7/IV
(G Pedal)

IV$^6_4$ V7 (G Pedal)

| I | V | 7 | I | V | 7 | | I |

The V/V chord, while common in the major key, is less frequently found in minor. There, the unaltered II₇ is sometimes preferred to its alteration as a V/V. (Example 173.)

EXAMPLE 173

Cm: I   V   I   V⁷/V   V

Cm: I   V   I   II⁷   V

The V/VI chord is common when the sixth degree is lowered, and the chord is major. The triad on the raised sixth degree, however, is diminished, and is therefore not usually preceded by a secondary dominant. The effect is extremely intense. (Example 174.)

EXAMPLE 174

The same principle applies to both VII chords. That built on the lowered degree is major, and will appear following its dominant; that built on the raised degree is diminished, as it is also in major. (Example 175.)

EXAMPLE 175

This, then, concludes our survey of the most familiar secondary dominant chords in the major and minor keys. One can find examples of their use in all the music of the standard repertoire. One can even find passages in which secondary dominants follow in continual succession. The theoretical basis behind a series of these consecutive chords is easy to find. If E is the dominant of A, A in turn is the dominant of D, which is the dominant of G, etc. Thus, when we move an E_7 to A, we can follow that A chord by an A_7 and move it in turn to D, D_7, G, etc. (Example 176.)

EXAMPLE 176

Now, if we telescope this progression, and move the E_7 directly to A_7, we have heightened the tension of the passage, but in no way interfered with the root movement, which still ascends in 4ths. (Example 177.)

EXAMPLE 177

These chord sequences travel clockwise around the circle of fifths. If one continues far enough, one will eventually return to the opening chord.

The function of a secondary dominant should be clearly understood, and more weight should not be placed on it than it can bear. If a chord other than the tonic is preceded by its own dominant, then for that moment this chord or scale degree is strengthened or reinforced. This is not the same thing as a modulation to that area. Modulation is the technical term for a key change. When we modulate, we leave the original scale behind, and accept a new scale, a new keynote, and an entirely new set of chord relations. We traditionally modulate into a new key through its dominant, but we cannot say that the modulation has taken place until the new key has been firmly established. In most Classical music, the new key appears along with a new theme. We normally modulate from one key to another by the use of chords that are common to both keys. Thus, a type of transitional harmony is developed that could be interpreted in either of two keys, until finally the second key affirms itself through a strong emphasis on its dominant.

Let us make this distinction doubly clear. In order to strengthen the dominant area in the key of C, or to highlight an appearance of the dominant triad, we might introduce a V/V chord D-F♯-A-C. On the other hand, if we wish to modulate to the key of G, we will probably conclude our modulatory section with the same D₇ chord. This D₇, however, is no longer a V/V in C but rather a dominant in G. Example 178 shows parallel passages from a well-known sonata by Mozart which demonstrate this device perfectly.

EXAMPLE 178

b.

C: V   I$^6_4$ V   I$^6_4$ V

a. Allegro

G: I   IV$^6_4$ I   IV$^6_4$ I

In the first passage, we are modulating from C to G, and the modulatory passage is followed by a new theme in the key of G. In the repetition of this passage later in the movement, the same bars are followed by the same theme, but this time in the key of C. Once again we see that a chord progression can only be identified in relation to the music itself as it appears within the living composition.

The progression in example 179 would seem to be in the key of C.

EXAMPLE 179

C: D$^6_5$ G^7 C

Yet there is fundamentally nothing here that could not appear within the key of A minor, or G major, or F major, or E minor, or D minor. Can you construct a longer passage around these chords by placing chords before and after them that would place them in the various keys mentioned? Example 180 shows how this could be done.

It is the ambiguous quality of the individual chord that opens the door to the entire world of chromatic harmony. A chord or short progression will not in itself clarify the key, but may be capable of interpretation in a number of ways. Harmonies rooted to one point on the circle of fifths can easily move around that circle in either direction. What stabilizes a musical passage exclusively in the key of C is not so much the use of I-V-I progressions as the overcoming of those harmonies that might tend to move toward G or toward F. The structure of any musical composition, and a fundamental aspect of its

EXAMPLE 180

G: I   V$_7^{6-5}$ I   IV   *   V$_2^4$/IV   IV$_4^6$ V^7 I

C: D$_5^6$ G^7 C

*If the G^7 chord in the following bar is considered a dominant of C (V/IV), then this D^7 chord could be called a subdominant of C (IV/IV).

style, can always be seen in the way in which the key is established, the way in which antitonic elements are introduced, and finally the way in which these elements are overcome.

Define:
  Secondary dominant chord
  Modulation
  Cross relationship

INDEX

INDEX